# Brain Power

# What's the Big Idea?

## 2,400,000 Years of Inventions

David Stewart

D1579420

FERBANE

18 NOV 2023

WITHDRAWN

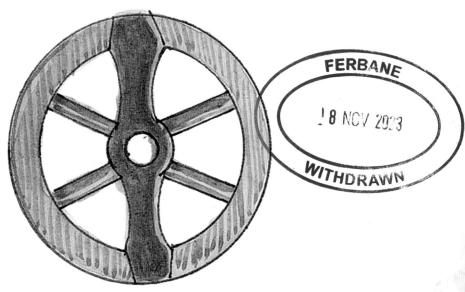

BOOK HOUSE

Leabharlann
Chontae Uíbh Fhailí

Class:
Acc:
Inv:

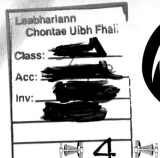

# Contents

Due to the changing nature of internet links, Book House has developed an online list of websites related to the subject of this book. This site is updated regularly. Please use this link to access the list:
**http://www.book-house.co.uk/bp/bigidea**

# EARLY PEOPLE

Imagine the scene: a crouching figure is bashing open a bone with a stone. As the bone splits the stone chips and nicks his finger. Licking off the blood he thinks: "If a stone can cut me it can cut other things too!"

Was this how our Stone Age ancestors started using stone tools as knives some 600,000 years ago? If so, knives are discoveries rather than inventions. But there was nothing accidental about bows and arrows, first used in Africa about 30,000 BC. It probably took many years to learn which woods and fibres made the most effective weapons.

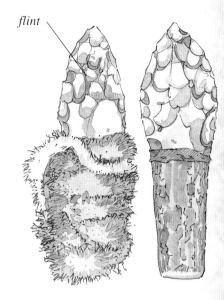

flint

Flint is easily chipped to make a razor-sharp edge. In the Stone Age most knives were made of flint.

## What's the big idea? FAST FOOD!

heave!

Whooosh!

thump!

snap!

crack!

*Stone Age humans are nomadic hunters, chasing wild beasts over vast, open plains. They use spears, bows and arrows, sticks and slings to bring down their prey from a safe distance.*

*Humans catch mammoths by organised hunting. First they cover a deep pit with branches and grass, then they chase the weakest animal in the herd into the trap where they kill it with stones and spears.*

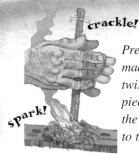

*crackle!*

*Prehistoric man made fire by rapidly twisting a stick on a piece of wood until the friction set light to tinder.*

*spark!*

# Inventions

**2,400,000 BC** A stone sharpened for cutting is one of the first inventions. One end has a point or cutting edge and the other end is rounded so it is comfortable to hold.

*stone*    *leather strip*

## Events

**750,000 BC** Hearths found in the Escale cave near Marseilles, France, show that *Homo erectus* (an early type of human) used fire.

**160,000 BC** The first modern humans (*Homo sapiens*) appear in Africa.

**70,000 BC** Modern humans start to leave Africa. They settle in Europe and South Asia.

**55,000 BC** The first people reach Australia. Within five thousand years they have wiped out many species there.

**47,000 BC** An asteroid 45 m across hits what is now known as Arizona, USA. It causes an explosion as big as 10 H-bombs which leaves the 1.5-km wide Meteor Crater.

**30,000 BC** Paleolithic peoples in Central Europe and France record numbers on tallies made of animal bones, ivory and stone.

**25,000 BC** Humans in France produce music.

**12,000 BC** The earliest evidence of people living in North America.

*chip chip*

**250,000 BC** Stone axes in use in Europe, Asia and Africa. The axe head is bound to a wooden handle with leather strips. An axe with a handle can be swung with greater force than one without, so makes a better tool.

**50,000 BC** People are painting pictures in caves in the Middle East, Europe and Africa. They make paints from coloured muds and rocks. Many of the paintings show hunting scenes. The caves are dark so the artists need lamps to do their painting. The oldest known lamp is 17,000 years old and was found in France where there are many cave paintings. It is made from a hollowed-out stone which held a lump of animal fat with a moss wick.

*spray painting with a hollow reed*

*animal fat*

*moss wick*

**8000 BC** Fish traps catch more fish than a line or spear. The traps, woven from wooden rods and twigs, are put across the mouths of streams.

*cane trap*

5

# THE FIRST CITIES

Some time around 8000 BC the Sumerians, a nomadic hunting tribe in what we now call the Middle East, gradually settled and began farming. They built villages along river banks and the first cities developed from these villages. The Sumerians also founded several city-states in ancient Mesopotamia (now Iraq). The cities' rulers developed systems of government and collected taxes to pay for public buildings and irrigation systems. They recorded the tax payments in the earliest-known form of writing, called 'cuneiform'.

## What's the big idea? WHEELS

Solid wheel

Plank wheel

Semi solid

Spoked wheel

*The first wheels were solid discs of wood cut from tree trunks. Then came wheels of wooden planks held together with wood or metal brackets. These wheels were heavy, so sections of wood were cut out to lighten them. More and more wood was cut away until the spoked wheel, which we still use, appeared around 2000 BC.*

## Domesticating animals

The dog was the first animal to be domesticated, but what about the others? Perhaps hunters caught young animals to rear for food. Certainly by 9000 BC people in Turkey were keeping pigs, and by 8000 BC large flocks of sheep and goats were common throughout the Middle East. Cattle were next, and by 2000 BC camels and horses had also been domesticated.

SQUEAL!
**OINK!**
GRUNT!

*He doesn't sound very domesticated!*

## Events

**11,000 to 9500 BC** The ice sheets covering northern America, Europe and Asia melt and the last ice age ends.

**7000 BC** The first walled settlements appear at Jericho in the Middle East.

**5600 BC** Rising sea levels cause the Mediterranean Sea to break through a natural dam at the Bosphorus in Turkey, and flood into the Black Sea, which was then just a freshwater lake.

**c. 5500 BC** Farmers begin growing rice in the valley of the Yellow River in eastern China.

**5000 BC** Rising sea levels cover the land bridge between Britain and Europe.

**5000 BC** The first city-state is founded in Mesopotamia (Iraq).

**c. 3000 BC** People living in the valley of the River Indus (in modern Pakistan) use cotton to make clothes.

**c. 2500 BC** Farmers high in the Andes Mountains in Peru, South America, are growing potatoes. Pottery and metal working skills also spread among farming communities.

# Inventions

*pot made from wet clay coils*

**7000 BC** The first simple pots are shaped from coils of wet clay in the area of the Middle East now known as Turkey.

*If only this wheel moved more easily...*

**3500 BC** The first wheel appears in Mesopotamia. This is the potter's wheel – a circular table which spins while a potter works clay on it.

*early potter's wheel*

**3500 BC** Bronze, a mixture of copper and tin, is discovered. Molten bronze is poured into a mould and allowed to cool before being used.

*molten bronze*

*mould*

**3500 BC** Writing is invented in Sumer. Simple pictures are used for words and marked on soft clay with a reed stylus. This form of writing, known as 'cuneiform', is soon used all over the Middle East.

*cuneiform*

*clay*

**2000 BC** Horses are tamed, but cannot pull heavy loads because the harness chokes them. It will be 200 years before chariots are light enough for horses to pull. And it will be many more centuries before the harness is really improved.

*...200 years later...*

*If you ask me, life was easier before they improved the harness!*

## The first farmers

Hunting and gathering were the main ways of finding food before the development of farming. Hunter-gatherers usually lived in groups of a few dozen and had to keep moving as food supplies ran out. Farming evolved as hunter-gatherers used their knowledge of plants to grow and harvest them in an organised way. Farming also meant domesticating animals for their produce. Changes in the climate may have forced people to settle in one place. They began to settle where there was a regular water supply. They could now live together in larger groups, and because they had a regular

**A Sumerian dairy scene**

supply of food they had time to learn other skills – pottery, weaving and metalworking for tools and weapons. And because they were not always on the move they could build permanent homes.

7

# ANCIENT EGYPT

Ancient Egypt was one of the world's great civilisations. The Egyptians produced marvellous works of art and architecture. They studied mathematics, astronomy and medicine and invented a form of writing using pictures called hieroglyphics. The farming communities that had developed along the banks of the River Nile since before 5000 BC grew into the two kingdoms of Upper and Lower Egypt. Then, in 3118 BC, they were united into one kingdom by Menes, the first Egyptian pharaoh.

## Events

**2550 BC** Work starts on the Great Pyramid at Giza. It takes 30 years to build.

**2075 BC** The giant 'sarsen' stones, each weighing 25 tonnes, are erected at Stonehenge in what is now Wiltshire, England.

**1628 BC** The volcanic island of Thera explodes. This creates gigantic waves up to 50 m tall that devastate the Minoan civilisation on the nearby island of Crete.

**1400 BC** Warriors from Mycenae invade Greece. Their settlements will develop into the Greek civilisation.

**1200 BC** The Trojan War is fought in western Anatolia, present-day Turkey.

**800 BC** The Greek poet Homer writes the *Iliad* and the *Odyssey*, legends of the Trojan War and what happened afterwards.

**776 BC** The first Olympic Games are held.

**449 BC** The 40-year long war between the Persians and Greeks ends with the Greek navy's victory at Salamis.

## What's the big idea? PYRAMIDS

*The pyramids were built as tombs for the pharaohs, the rulers of Egypt. Their shape represented the rays of the sun falling on the earth. The Egyptians believed that when the pharaoh died he climbed to heaven on the sun's rays. The pyramids were built with amazing accuracy for such huge structures. This precison was due to the measuring and building tools the Egyptian builders developed.*

A lot of blooming work for a tomb!

Argh!

It's not just a tomb - it's a stairway to heaven!

*EGYPTIAN TOOLS*

right angle

scissors

plumb line

ruler

thud

chip

# Inventions

## The Egyptians measure time

### 3000 BC
The Egyptians invent hieroglyphics, a way of writing with pictures to represent words, syllables and sounds. After the invention of papyrus (an early paper), the symbols are changed so they can be written more quickly. This is the beginning of our system of writing.

*Dear mum, The weather's fine...*

*long wooden pole*
*weight*
*bucket*

### 2500 BC
The invention of the *shaduf* makes watering crops easier. It is a long wooden pole with a weight on one end. On the other end is a bucket which is lowered into the river to fill with water before it is pulled up by the weight.

### 2000 BC
The Egyptians invent the shadow clock. The shadow of the cross-bar falls on a scale which shows the time. Each morning the clock is pointed east into the sun. In the afternoon the clock is pointed west.

*shadow showing time*

### 700 BC
King Gyges of Lydia (in present-day Turkey) issues the first-known coins. Made from a mixture of gold and silver, they have a picture of the king stamped on one side.

*potter's kick wheel*

*It just needed a good kick!*

### 300 BC
The potter's kick wheel is being used by the Greeks and Egyptians. The potter keeps the pot turning by kicking on a heavy wheel at the bottom.

The Ancient Egyptians were the first to establish the length of a year, possibly because the River Nile floods every year. This flood almost always coincided with the date that the Sun and the star Sirius rose together in the sky. Although there are 365 days between such risings, a year is about a quarter of a day longer than 365 days. As a result the Egyptians' calendar went in and out of alignment with the seasons over a period of about 1455 years, but it accurately matched the seasons with dates in AD 139. Knowing this, modern astronomers believe that the Egyptians were using the 365-day year as early as 4228 BC.

*an Egyptian astronomer*

### Later the Greeks take the 'leap'...
Greek astronomers added the missing quarter day to the Egyptian calendar by adding an extra (leap) day every four years, but most people ignored it. The Greek system was adopted by the Romans under Julius Caesar in 46 BC.

9

# THE ANCIENT GREEKS

## SLAVES

They need to invent a machine to do this...

Why bother when they have us?

The Greeks were full of ideas, but hardly invented anything to make life easier. They didn't need to – like other ancient civilizations they had slaves to do all the hard work.

You would not be reading this book if it had not been for the Ancient Greeks. They developed the first proper alphabet (the word comes from *alpha* and *beta,* the first two letters of their alphabet). And, amazingly, the ideas of the Ancient Greeks still influence the way Europeans think about politics, science, education and the arts. Greek architecture, writing and theatre have inspired people from the Ancient Romans to the present day, but perhaps the most important of all Greek ideas was democracy. This was the idea that all citizens should have a say in how their city was run. *Demokratia* is a Greek word meaning 'rule by the people'.

We can solve our problems by discussion - not by fighting!

The citizens of Athens held an assembly every nine days. Only about 5000 citizens attended regularly. Meetings were often noisy and argumentative.

## What's the big idea? DEMOCRACY
(but only for some...)

Athens was the largest of the Greek city-states with a population of 260,000 at its peak. But only the 45,000 or so male citizens were allowed to vote. There was no vote for women, people born outside Athens or the city's 70,000 slaves.

Athens is home to 260,000 people. That makes us the largest democracy in Greece!

Yes, but 215,000 of them aren't allowed to vote!

# Inventions

**285 BC** King Ptolemy II builds the first lighthouse near the Egyptian city of Alexandria. Called the Pharos, it is over 130 m high. It is lit by fire at the top, which is kept burning all night.

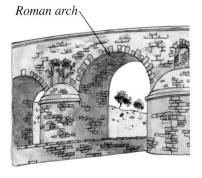

**250 BC** The Archimedean screw is a tube containing a spiral with a handle at one end. When the lower end of the tube is put in water and the handle turned, the spiral carries the water up the tube so it flows out at the top. The screw is a very simple machine, but it makes raising water much easier.

**250 BC** The Greek inventor Ctesibius of Alexandria, Egypt, invents the suction pump. It uses air pressure to suck up water when the handle at the top is rocked backwards and forwards.

*Roman arch*

**200 BC** The Romans build the first arched bridge. The invention of the arch makes a huge difference to the building of houses and bridges. Before the arch, buildings could only use horizontal beams supported by vertical pillars.

**150 BC** The first true paper is made in China. Cloth, wood and straw are beaten to a pulp and mixed with water. Thin sheets are pressed flat and hung out to dry.

*paper-making in ancient China*

# Inventors

### Archimedes (287 to 212 BC)

Archimedes, born in Syracuse, Italy, was one of the most important people in the development of mathematics. He also invented several clever devices. As well as the Archimedean screw, he invented things that used pulleys for extra pulling force. In 214 BC a Roman army attacked Archimedes' home city. The inventor used pulleys and levers to create giant claws and rams that destroyed many of the Roman ships. He is also said to have used mirrors to focus the sun's rays until they were hot enough to set fire to the enemy fleet. Despite these war machines, Syracuse eventually fell after a long siege. The Roman general ordered that Archimedes should be saved, but he was killed by a soldier who was unaware of who he was.

### Ctesibius (285 to 222 BC)

Ctesibius was the first person to prove that air was a material substance and that it could create a pushing or pulling force under pressure. In addition to the first suction pump, he invented a water clock that was the most accurate way of keeping time until the seventeenth century.

# THE ROMANS

In the eighth century BC a tribe of people we now call 'Latins' settled beside the River Tiber in Italy. They built a village of reed huts. Gradually this grew into a town and then into Rome – the capital of the Roman Empire. This great empire, which lasted nearly a thousand years, was most powerful under the emperors Trajan (AD 98-117) and Hadrian (AD 117-138). The Romans conquered the Greeks and developed many of their ideas. They were also superb engineers, building roads, bridges, harbours and aqueducts. Without these they could not have run their huge empire.

## Events

**73 BC** Spartacus leads a rebellion of fellow slaves against Rome. Defeated in 70 BC, 6000 of the rebels are crucified as punishment.

**27 BC** The reign of the first Roman emperor, Augustus Caesar, begins.

**AD 43** Britain becomes the province of Britannia after its conquest by the Romans.

**AD 248** Rome celebrates its 1000th anniversary.

**AD 476** The city of Rome is overrun by the Goths.

## What's the big idea? CONCRETE

Builders in Mesopotamia and Ancient Egypt used early forms of concrete, but the Romans developed it into a really useful material. They made a new, better kind of concrete by adding a special volcanic ash (polozza) to the original ingredients: lime, water and lumps of stone. The new concrete was waterproof and much stronger. Now it was possible to build concrete structures that were stronger, lighter and cheaper than those made of stone.

*In 19 BC the Pont du Gard, in Nîmes, France, is built. It is 49 m high and supplies each citizen with about 600 litres of water a day. Without such a good water supply the city could not have developed.*

*This treadmill-powered crane has a pole with a pulley at the top. Turning the wheel or treadmill at the bottom lifts the weight at the top.*

*The first walls the Romans built were of rubble bonded with clay and limestone (1). Later they used rubble and cement (2). They faced outside walls with limestone (3) or small square stones (4) and used layers (courses) of brick and stone (5) at the corners. Inside, partition walls were made of timber-framed rubble (6).*

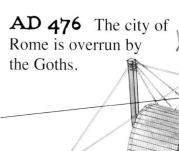

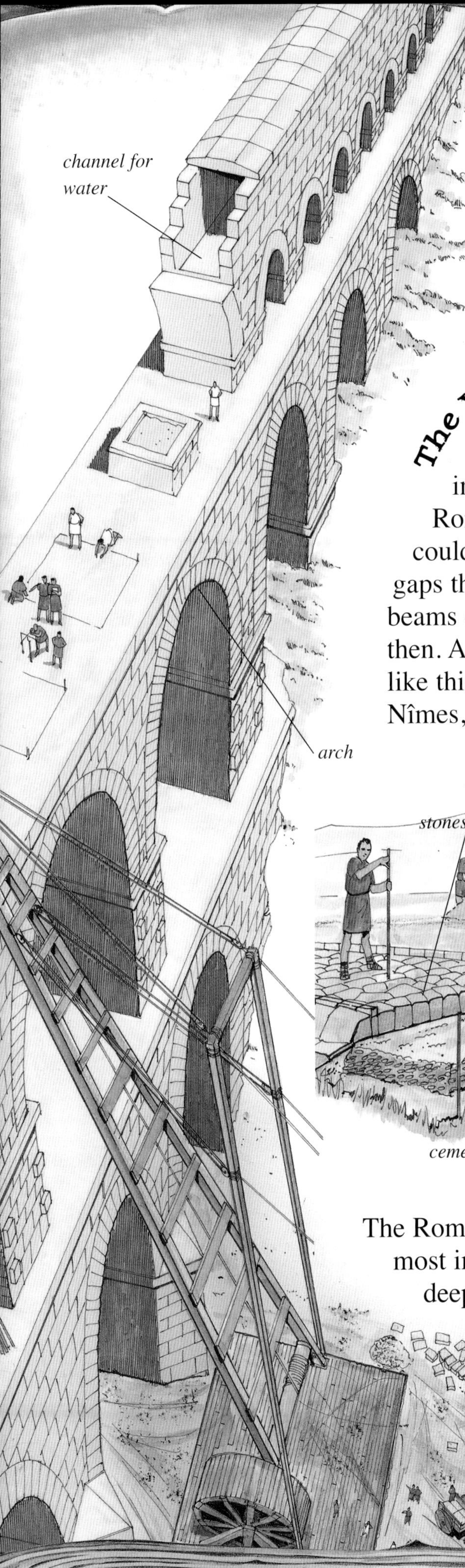

_channel for water_

_channel_

"Warmth, at last! It's so cold in Britannia."

_hot air_

_furnace_

"Now if only we could stop it raining every day..."

_channel_

## The vaulted arch

Arches, invented by the Romans in 200 BC, could span much larger gaps than the horizontal beams on posts used before then. Arches made projects like this huge aqueduct at Nîmes, France, possible.

_arch_

The Romans were the first to develop central heating. Heat from a furnace passed along channels under the floors and up the brick walls of houses. This skill was lost when the western part of the Roman Empire collapsed.

## Roman roads

_stones_

_groma_

_kerbstones_

_concrete_

_ditch_

_cement_

_sand_

The Romans built 80,000 km of roads across their empire. The most important roads were made by digging a trench with deeper drainage ditches on each side. Then they put down a layer of sand followed by a layer of cement, a layer of concrete and finally a top surface of stone slabs with kerbstones at the sides. The Roman engineers used a surveying instrument called a groma to help construct straight lines, rectangles and squares.

13

# THE DARK AGES

After invaders captured Rome in AD 476 the Roman Empire finally collapsed.

*Well, for one thing I can tell you that it wasn't dark!*

In western Europe the peace and order of Roman rule was replaced by invasions and uncertainty and the period is often called the 'Dark Ages'. The Vikings and Anglo-Saxons of northern Europe began to run out of land as their populations increased, so they invaded Britain and western Europe. The Vikings were brilliant sailors and explorers, settling in Russia and lands that no European had seen before – including North America. But not everywhere was unsettled. By the seventh century the Arab world was thriving. The Byzantine Empire (the eastern half of the old Roman Empire) was technologically advanced and very powerful for more than 800 years after Rome collapsed.

Great civilisations flourished in Mexico, India and China. Some important Chinese inventions from this time (for example porcelain) were unknown in Europe for several hundred years.

## Events

**AD 632** Mohammed, the first prophet of Islam, dies.

**AD 673-8** The Arabs besiege Constantinople, the capital of the Byzantine Empire. They are beaten off when the defenders shoot 'Greek Fire', a burning mixture of oils and other chemicals, at their ships.

**AD 715** The Moslem Empire stretches eastwards from the Pyrenees in Spain to western China.

**AD 800** Charlemagne becomes the first Holy Roman Emperor and rules much of western Europe.

## What's the big idea?
# AMERICA

*In 1000 Viking explorers find a country they call Vinland. Today it is known as America.*

*Growl! You're too early – come back in 1492! (see p24)*

# Inventions

**c. AD 300** The Chinese invent stirrups. They had invented the padded saddle a century or so earlier. Together, stirrups and saddle give the rider a firm seat on the horse.

*Chinese horseman*

**1234 567 89**

**AD 500** The Arabs invent the numbers (digits) we use today. These nine numbers can be arranged to give many other numbers.

**c. AD 850** King Alfred the Great of England is said to invent the candle clock. A candle is marked with hours. As the candle burns down, the passing hours can be counted from the marks.

**c. AD 850** The Chinese invent porcelain, a tough, white, waterproof material made from clay. They use it for cups and vases. It will be 350 years before porcelain reaches Europe.

*Chinese porcelain*

*pages from the Diamond Sutra*

**AD 868** The first printed book, the Diamond Sutra, is made in China. Printed with carved wooden blocks it shows scenes from the life of the Buddha, a religious leader.

**AD 950** The wheeled plough is invented in Europe. The two wheels at the front make the plough easier to use and guide.

With the collapse of the Roman Empire western Europe plunged into chaos, but in Arabia, far to the east, a new force was emerging. In AD 630 Mohammed, a religious preacher from Mecca (in modern Saudi Arabia) founded a holy state based on the rules of his new faith, Islam. The followers of Islam spread their influence across the Middle East, parts of Europe and Africa and soon controlled a vast empire.

Most of the ideas and technologies of the Greek and Roman civilisations were forgotten in the west. But many survived in the Middle East, which also benefited from trade with the great Indian and Chinese civilisations to the east.

During the period known as the Dark Ages the Arab civilisation was the most scientifically advanced in the world, particularly in astronomy and medicine. The techniques practised by doctors such as Rhazes (AD 850-932) were centuries in advance of those used in Europe. Arab doctors studied their patients carefully to discover the effects of disease. They also developed delicate instruments with which to perform operations. And Arab medicines were famous throughout the medieval world.

# THE EARLY MIDDLE AGES

The Christian church had started as a small persecuted sect in the Middle East. But by AD 1000 it dominated most of Europe. Throughout the Middle Ages the Church controlled every aspect of people's lives from education and holidays to law, literature and art. As time passed the Church gained more land and power, and in some places became corrupt. Anyone who questioned the authority of the Church was brutally punished. Many people became monks or nuns, devoting their lives to 'God's work'. They lived simply, working the land and praying in isolated communities called monasteries. (Communities of nuns were called convents.) Unlike most people of the time, many monks and nuns could read and write. Monasteries often had very old texts in their libraries which the monks carefully copied so they would not be lost. Without these copies many of the works by Ancient Greek and Roman authors that we know today would not have survived.

## What's the big idea? PRISON

Prisons did exist before the Middle Ages – but imprisonment was not usually regarded as a punishment. Instead prisons were used to keep people captive before they were executed or sent into slavery.

*Unfortunately!*

## Events

**1066** The Normans invade England and William the Conqueror becomes king.

**1086** The Domesday book is produced. It contains details of all landholdings and livestock in England.

**1150** Angkor Wat, a gigantic temple complex, is built in Cambodia. It covers 81 hectares and is surrounded by a moat of 19 km.

**1175** Saladin, a Muslim Kurd, comes to power in Syria and Egypt. He conquers Jerusalem and founds an Arab empire.

**1200** Manco Capac, leader of the Incas, founds the sacred city of Cuzco in Peru.

**1204** An army of Christian Crusaders captures and loots the Christian city of Constantinople (modern Istanbul, Turkey).

**1215** King John of England is forced to sign the Magna Carta, a code of conduct drawn up by a committee of noblemen to end corruption.

**1218** The Mongols (nomadic warriors from Central Asia) start moving westwards.

# Inventions

**C. 1100** The magnetic compass (right) is invented by the Chinese.

**1200** The Arabs make advanced astrolabes (left), mechanical devices showing the position of certain stars on any given date and at any given time. This helps navigation.

**1250** The longbow is invented in Wales. It is very powerful and bowmen can fire it much more quickly than the crossbow.

*musical notes*

**1260** For the first time European musical notation is marked to show different pitches. Symbols to show the length of sounds are added around 1260.

**C. 1286** Spectacles (below) are invented in Italy. They start becoming popular in the early 1300s.

*early spectacles*

*Windmills with horizontal sails were probably invented in Persia about AD 700. Windmills with vertical sails were being used in Europe by 1200.*

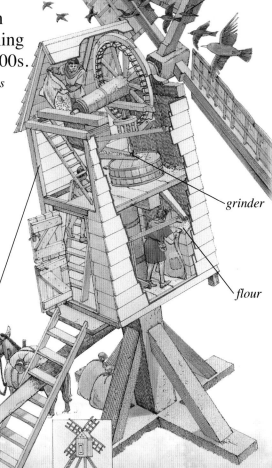

*longbow*

*sails*

*grinder*

*flour*

## The flying buttress

The first churches were simple structures of wood or other cheap materials. As the Church became richer, stone churches were built all over Europe to display the power of the Christian faith. As churches got bigger, building techniques had to change to ensure the churches did not collapse – some did. This building boom reached its height with the construction of vast cathedrals during the

**Flying buttresses on a cathedral**

Middle Ages. Churchmen wanted big beautiful buildings, but as the cathedrals got bigger and wider, the strain on their walls become enormous. The flying buttress was developed to overcome the need to build thick, ugly walls. Flying buttresses use stone arches to transfer some of the strain from the wall to thick pillars set some distance from it, to create a structure that is both strong and elegant.

# CASTLES AT WAR

Throughout the Middle Ages, Europe was often convulsed by war as rulers grabbed land or riches from neighbouring states. To protect their lands or to control new conquests, kings and nobles built castles. Hundreds of castles were built all over Europe during the Middle Ages. The first ones were wooden, but these were soon replaced by strong stone ones. Castles were built on sites that were easy to defend, such as hilltops, or in important places, such as by river crossings or roads. A castle also showed its owner's power and wealth.

*Many enemy castles were captured by siege. Attacking forces surrounded ('besieged') the castle to cut off its food and water supplies so that its inhabitants starved. A siege might last months, but could be shortened by using siege engines – giant wooden machines designed to destroy a castle's defences. Battering rams broke through heavy doors, mangonels and trebuchets hurled huge rocks to smash castle walls, while siege towers helped the attackers to get closer to the walls.*

siege tower

digging a tunnel to undermine the castle walls

battering ram

## Armour

In the early Middle Ages soldiers had worn chain mail for protection. Made of metal rings linked together, it was easily pierced by sword points and arrows. Later, metal plates were added for extra protection. Eventually whole suits were made of these plates. They gave excellent protection, but were so expensive only knights (rich warriors employed by rulers) could afford them.

# Inventions

**C. 1300** Adaptations to the caravel, a small Mediterranean trading ship, would lead to it becoming the ship used by Spanish and Portuguese explorers.

What's the **big** idea?

## GUNPOWDER

*A Chinese cannon of about 1324. The Chinese invented gunpowder around 1000.*

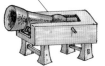

**1346** The Battle of Crécy, France, and the first-known use of cannons in Europe. Edward II of England uses them against the French, but the English longbowmen probably contribute more to the victory than the cannons. Heavy and difficult to manoeuvre, cannons are more useful against the walls of a castle or town. Early cannons fire stone-shot – iron cannonballs will not be invented until about 1400. Castle walls cannot withstand cannon fire, so castles are no longer any use as defences.

*mangonel*

*trebuchet*

**1364** Giovanni de' Dondi makes a clock with seven faces to show the position of each of the then known planets. It is the most complicated clock yet made.

# FEUDAL SOCIETY

In medieval Europe kings and other rulers owned most of the land. They gave some to loyal noblemen who helped them control their territory. These nobles gave land to knights (warriors of noble birth) in return for help in times of trouble. Some people, called freemen, were skilled in different crafts or trades that gave them some control of their lives. Most people were powerless peasants who worked the land for nobles and knights in return for a share of the crop. This 'feudal' system was the basis of European society throughout the Middle Ages. A similar system developed in Japan at this time. Elsewhere in the world other powerful states emerged, including the Aztecs and Incas in America, the kingdom of Mali in Africa and the Mongols in Asia.

## What's the big idea? CATHEDRALS TOUCH THE SKY

*Cathedrals were meant to be noticed. They were built as monuments to the greatness of God, but they also brought glory to the men who built them and to the towns in which they stood. Flying buttresses supported these big buildings, but to make them even more impressive, towers or spires were often added. These 'fingers' (spires) pointed to heaven and served as a constant reminder of God. Cathedrals with spires remained the tallest buildings in Europe until the nineteenth century. Although many medieval cathedrals have been damaged by war or natural disasters such as lightning or earthquakes, those that survive are still some of the world's largest and most impressive buildings.*

Cathedrals can soar even higher with flying buttresses (p. 17).

# Inventions

This alphabet dates from the Middle Ages. It has 24 letters, two less than today's alphabet – there is no J or V.

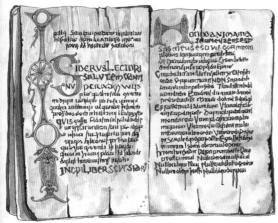

Writing and producing books in medieval Europe is dominated by the Christian church. All books have to be copied out by hand and it can take a monk 20 or 30 years to copy out one bible or prayer book.

**C. 1380** The colour of a patient's urine is widely used to diagnose illness. By the fifteenth century it has become a highly sophisticated technique.

*A uroscopy chart is used to match the colour of a patient's urine with an illness.*

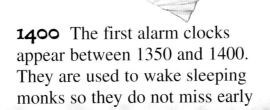

**1400** The first alarm clocks appear between 1350 and 1400. They are used to wake sleeping monks so they do not miss early morning prayers.

# Events

**1295** Venetian trader Marco Polo returns home after 17 years at the court of the Emperor Kublai Khan in China. Europeans know very little about this great civilisation.

**1347** The Black Death (bubonic plague) reaches Europe. The first outbreak began in China and spread west along trade routes. In 1348 it reaches England and France and by 1351 has affected most of Europe. The disease is carried by rats and spreads to people when they are bitten by fleas that live on the infected animals. Buboes (big black swellings) appear in the armpits or groin of those infected and most victims die in two or three days. The disease will kill about 25 million people in Europe, a quarter of the population. This disaster causes so much social and economic upheaval that it takes 100 years for Europe to recover.

AAARGH!

# THE RENAISSANCE

T he Middle Ages did not have an exact end. Instead many things combined to end the feudal system on which medieval society had been based. One was the Black Death (plague), which had killed millions of people in the fourteenth century. This caused a shortage of workers and pushed up wages. Another was increased trade which made some cities very rich and good places to work. Around this time Italian scholars began exploring the ideas of the early classical Greek and Roman writers. The Christian church controlled everything in people's lives, but the classical writers encouraged people to think for themselves. Soon art and philosophy were flourishing and there was new interest in scientific observation. Later, historians would call this return to classical ideas a 'renaissance', or rebirth.

## What's the big idea? PRINTING BOOKS

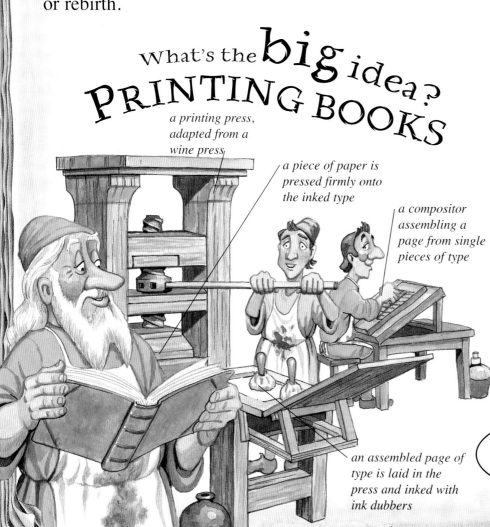

a printing press, adapted from a wine press

a piece of paper is pressed firmly onto the inked type

a compositor assembling a page from single pieces of type

an assembled page of type is laid in the press and inked with ink dubbers

## Events

**1415** 12,000 English soldiers face a French army of 60,000 at Agincourt – the longbow wins the battle for the English.

**1441** Jan van Eyck, a Flemish artist, is believed to be the first to use oil paints. These give a richer, more glowing effect than previous techniques.

**1453** Constantinople falls to the Turks. This is the end of the Byzantine Empire which had lasted nearly a thousand years and grew from the eastern part of the old Roman Empire.

**1470** The Inca Empire in South America reaches its greatest extent, stretching 4000 km from Colombia in the north to Chile in the south. The emperor rules about 10 million people.

**1477** In a huge sacrifice to the gods in Tenochtitlán, the capital of the Aztec Empire (in what is now Mexico), the Aztec emperor and his councillors cut the hearts out of 20,000 captives with flint knives.

Have a heart! Just not mine, please!

# Inventions

# Gutenberg

**1450** In Germany playing cards (above) are printed with wooden blocks. The first cards were used in China around AD 850. The four suits appeared in 1440.

**1452** Birth of Leonardo da Vinci, who will be one of the great figures of the Renaissance. Among his inventions will be an odometer, a device to measure distance travelled. It uses a system of gears to display the distance accurately.

**1492** The first globe is constructed by German map-maker Martin Brehaim. It is very inaccurate and does not show America, which will remain unknown to Renaissance Europeans until later this year.

**1498** Toothbrushes with bristles at right angles to the handle are described in a Chinese encyclopedia.

**1538** The first recorded use of a diving bell is in Toledo, Spain. Edmund Halley, an English scientist, will develop his version (right) in 1717.

*I hope there aren't any sharks...*

*wooden case*

*graphite*

**1565** Konrad von Gesner, a Swiss doctor, invents the pencil. It has a centre of pure graphite (a soft black form of carbon) surrounded by wood.

Johannes Gutenberg (1397-1468), a German metalworker, revolutionised printing. He developed a way of casting individual metal letters and setting them into pages in the required order. This is called movable type and was first invented in China. However, because the Chinese alphabet has thousands of characters, the technology was not practical. The western alphabet, with only 26 letters, is much more suitable for this method of printing.

Gutenberg adapted a wine press to press sheets of paper against the ink-covered letters. The first book made with his printing press was a version of the Bible in 1454. By the end of the century thousands of printing presses were in operation and for the first time books became cheap and widely available. This helped spread the ideas and discoveries of the Renaissance around Europe.

# NEW HORIZONS

Medieval Europeans knew little about the rest of the world. Anything they knew about Asia and Africa was based on the tales of Arab traders and most people thought the world was flat. This changed dramatically in the fifteenth century. Portuguese explorers wanted to find a sea route to the Indies, the islands in southeast Asia where the valuable spices used to preserve and flavour foods were grown. Some explorers had reached the Indies by sailing east around Africa and across the Indian Ocean. Others believed it would be better (and quite safe) to sail westward because it was now known that the world was round.

Christopher Columbus led a Spanish expedition that sailed west. He found land, which became known as America. Within a century Spain and Portugal had conquered huge areas of it and were the richest countries in Europe.

## What's the big idea?
## LEONARDO DA VINCI
### invented almost everything!

What else can I have a go at?

*Aside from being a painter and inventor Leonardo da Vinci worked in many other fields, too:*
*astronomy*
*sculpture*
*geology*
*mathematics*
*botany*
*animal behaviour*
*engineering*
*architecture and music.*

## Events

**1492** Christopher Columbus reaches land after sailing west across the Atlantic. He thinks he has reached the Indies – islands in southeast Asia. But in fact he and his crew are the first Europeans to sight America in nearly 500 years (see pages 14-15).

**1522** A ship from the fleet of explorer Ferdinand Magellan returns home to Seville, Spain. It is the first vessel to sail around the world. Magellan himself was killed in the Philippines.

**1534** The Pope refuses to let Henry VIII of England divorce his wife, Catherine of Aragon. Henry breaks away from the Catholic Church in Rome and declares himself head of the Church of England.

Off with her head!

**1543** Astronomer Nicolaus Copernicus suggests that the sun, not the earth, is the centre of the universe.

**1552** Ivan the Terrible of Russia brings an end to the Mongol Empire.

# Inventions

Are we there yet?

## Leonardo da Vinci

**C. 1575** Stage wagons are large vehicles pulled by several horses. Slow and uncomfortable, they are used by poor people and to transport goods. The name comes from the stages of the wagon's journey, which are usually overnight stops at inns. First used in the fifteenth century, these wagons are common by the end of the next century.

**C. 1589** William Lee, an English church minister, invents the first mechanical knitting machine. The machine makes material from thread as fine as silk, ten times faster than a handknitter.

**1589** John Harrington, godson of Queen Elizabeth I of England, invents the flush toilet. It is installed in his home in Somerset, in the west of England, but it will not become popular for another 300 years.

*flush*

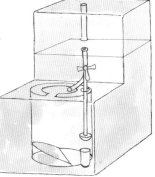

**1590** The first microscope with two lenses (a compound microscope) is made, probably by Dutch spectacle-maker Hans Janssen. But the technology for making lenses is not very good and so the microscope only gives rather blurred images.

If one man represents the spirit of the Renaissance it is Leonardo da Vinci (1452-1519). The Italian artist, scientist and inventor not only painted the Mona Lisa, one of the most famous works of art in the world, but he also studied mathematics, engineering and the workings of the human body.

Leonardo made thousands of sketches of his mechanical and structural ideas. These included designs for a huge variety of inventions: among them a submarine, an armoured tank, a digging machine, a diving mask and a steam engine.

He was fascinated by flight and spent a great deal of time studying birds and their movements. As a result he developed ideas for flying machines, such as an ornithopter, which used wings that flapped like a bird, a glider and an early helicopter. Leonardo's flying machines, along with many of his other inventions, were centuries ahead of their time. The technology to produce and power them did not exist, so most were never built.

25

# PARTICLES AND PLANETS

At this time no one understood how the human body worked. Most ideas were based on knowledge from Greek and Roman times, much of which was wrong. By the seventeenth century the centre of scientific learning had moved from Italy to northern Europe. Old ideas were challenged by people like William Harvey (1578-1657), an English doctor who was the first to describe the circulation of blood around the body. Harvey, like other researchers at this time, began to rely on his own observation, even if it contradicted the teachings of the time.

This change of attitude led to great advances in scientific knowledge – and underpins all scientific work. The work of Harvey and his fellow scientists was helped by the invention of new instruments. The microscope and telescope opened up new horizons of discovery, revealing tiny microbes and giant planets.

## Events

**1572** The last Inca ruler is executed by the Spanish who accuse him of encouraging paganism.

**1588** The Spanish Armada is defeated by a smaller, but more manoeuvrable, English fleet. The Spanish lose 65 ships – the English lose none.

**1600** American Indians of the Great Plains steal horses from Spanish settlers. They quickly learn to breed the horses and become highly skilled riders.

**1609** William Shakespeare publishes his sonnets.

**1619** A Dutch trader brings the first slaves from Africa to North America. By the time the trade is banned in 1808 12 million slaves will have been taken to the Americas.

**1648** The English Civil War ends with King Charles I's royalists being defeated by Oliver Cromwell's more efficient New Model Army. Charles I is beheaded in 1649.

**1660** The monarchy is restored as the reign of Charles II begins. Oliver Cromwell died in 1658 and his son Richard was too weak to retain power.

## What's the big idea? THE TELESCOPE

The Milky Way is a mass of innumerable stars planted together in clusters!

# Inventions

**1610**  The French invent the flintlock, a new mechanism for firing handguns. When the trigger is pulled a piece of flint (a type of rock) strikes a rough steel plate. This produces sparks which explode the gunpowder in the barrel, propelling the shot at the target.

**1637**  The first water-proof umbrella is made for King Louis XIII of France.
The very first umbrellas were a Chinese invention which had reached Europe by the twelfth century.

*Ze British will love zis invention!*

**1644**  The Italian scientist Evangelista Torricelli makes the first barometer, a device to measure air pressure. The level of mercury in a glass tube rises and falls as the air pressure changes.

*mercury*

**1650**  Otto von Guericke, a German scientist, invents the air pump (right). He uses his invention to demonstrate that air pressure is a powerful force.

**1656**  Dutch mathematician Christiaan Huygens makes the first working pendulum clock. It gained or lost only five minutes a day. Earlier clocks gained or lost as much as an hour each day.

**1661**  The Bank of Stockholm is the first bank to issue banknotes.

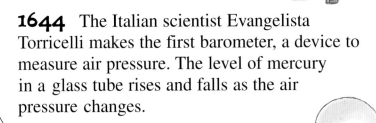

# Inventors

### Gerardus Mercator (1512-94)
In 1569 Gerardus Mercator, a Flemish cartographer (map-maker), invents a way of showing the round world on a flat piece of a paper. Known as 'Mercator's Projection', it allows navigators to plot an accurate course and is still used today.

### Galileo Galilei (1564-1642)
Born in Pisa, Italy, in 1609, Galilei makes a telescope and discovers Jupiter's moons with it. His discoveries support claims that the sun, not the earth, is the centre of the universe. In 1632 the Catholic Church challenges these claims, Galilei is arrested and his books banned.

### Blaise Pascal (1623-62)
A French mathematician, physicist and philosopher, Pascal invents a digital calculating machine, the syringe and the hydraulic press.

### Christiaan Huygens (1629-95)
Huygens devises a new technique for grinding lenses and uses them to create more accurate telescopes and discovers the rings of Saturn. Astronomical observations require accurate timekeeping and in 1656 Huygens invented the pendulum clock (left).

# Building Big Machines

Until the eighteenth century people only had wind, water or the muscles of horses, oxen or their own, to drive machines. But developments in engineering led to more complicated machines that needed more powerful sources of energy. A steam-driven device had been made by Hero, a Greek inventor, around 100 BC, but it was just a curiosity. The first practical steam-driven engine was invented in 1712 by Thomas Newcomen, an English blacksmith. Newcomen's engine converted energy from burning coal into an up-and-down movement to drive a pump. Now deep coal mines could be sunk, because any water flooding in could be pumped out. Steam power would make the Industrial Revolution possible and change the world forever.

What's the **big** idea? STEAM POWER

Thomas Newcomen's 1712 engine

## Events

**1665** The town of New York is founded on the island of Manhattan after an English fleet captures it from the Dutch.

**1680** The dodo, a large flightless bird living only on the island of Mauritius, is hunted to extinction by visiting sailors less than 80 years after its discovery.

**1705** Englishman Edmund Halley notices that a comet has been sighted at 76-year intervals throughout history and argues that it is the same comet each time. He predicts that it will return in 1758. It does – although Halley doesn't live to see it.

**1737** Swedish botanist Carl Linnaeus creates the first scientific system for classifying living things. It is a 'binomial' (two-name) system. Each plant and animal has a species name and a genus name. This system is still used today by scientists.

**1748** The Roman city of Pompeii, destroyed in AD 79 by a volcanic eruption, is partly excavated.

**1752** Britain finally adopts the Gregorian calendar, like the rest of Europe.

# Inventions

**1670** A French monk, Dom Perignon, invents champagne. He had put wine in tightly corked bottles while it was still fermenting and this made it fizzy. The wine 'tasted like stars' said Dom Perignon.

**1675** Christiaan Huygens makes another improvement to timekeeping. He adds a spring to the balance wheel, so it rocks back and forth, regulating the watch as it does so.

**1679** French scientist Denis Papin invents the pressure cooker. It is a cast-iron pot with an air-tight lid which allows liquids to boil at a higher temperature than normal.

**1701** English farmer Jethro Tull invents the seed drill. It sows seed in straight lines, so making it possible to weed between the rows and get better crops.

**1711** In London, John Shore, an instrument-maker, invents the tuning fork. This produces a musical note of a known pitch.

**1718** James Puckle, a London lawyer, demonstrates the first machine gun – it fires 63 bullets in 7 minutes.

**1752** Benjamin Franklin, the American scientist and statesman, invents the lightning conductor.

# Inventors

### Antoine van Leeuwenhoek (1632-1723)
The Dutchman Leeuwenhoek had no higher education but even so revolutionised biology with his invention of the first powerful microscope. It could magnify objects up to 200 times and people saw protozoa and bacteria for the first time. This would help in the discovery of what caused diseases.

### Isaac Newton (1642-1727)
One of the greatest scientists of all time, Englishman Newton was the first to realise there was a force of attraction between objects – gravity. He also discovered that white light could be split into a spectrum of coloured light, and suggested that light was made up of tiny particles. In 1666 he devised a new branch of mathematics – calculus.

### Thomas Newcomen (1663-1728)
In 1712 Englishman Newcomen invented the first practical steam-powered engine. It used steam to create a vacuum that allowed the pressure of the atmosphere to power a piston which then moved a pump shaft, allowing water to be pumped up from deep mines. Newcomen did not patent his device and received little money from it.

# NEW STEAM POWER

**B**y the 1730s, Thomas Newcomen's engines were at work in several countries throughout Europe. However, they were not the most energy-efficient machines and could only be used for pumping out mines. In the 1760s mathematician James Watt realised that the inefficiency of Newcomen's engine was because steam was condensed inside the engine cylinder. Every time cold water was injected to make the steam condense, it cooled the whole cylinder too, so the potential heat of the steam was wasted by cooling. Watt found this was the reason why engines used so much fuel and in 1782 he designed an engine with a separate condenser.

## What's the big idea? ENGINE EFFICIENCY

*Watt's machine condensed steam in a separate cylinder, a condenser, which he fitted next to the working cylinder, around which he fitted a steam jacket to keep it as hot as the steam that entered it.*

whirr!

click!

## Events

**1755** Much of the city of Lisbon in Portugal is destroyed by a massive earthquake. More than 10,000 people are killed by floods, fire and collapsing buildings.

**1777** Vermont is the first US state to abolish slavery.

**1779** British explorer Captain James Cook dies on the Pacific island of Hawaii in a skirmish with local people. Before his death he had surveyed much of Australasia and reached Antarctica.

**1782** William Herschel, a German amateur astronomer, discovers the planet Uranus. It is the first planet discovered since ancient times.

**1783** Britain recognises the independence of its former colonies in the United States.

**1789** George Washington becomes the first President of the United States of America.

**1791** African-American Benjamin Banneker invents an astronomical almanac.

**1789-92** The French Revolution results in the deaths of Louis XVI and Marie Antoinette and the founding of a republic.

# Inventions

**1757** Englishman John Campbell invents the sextant, an instrument which enables sailors to find their precise position at sea.

**1761** The Earl of Sandwich invents the sandwich so he can easily eat and gamble at the same time.

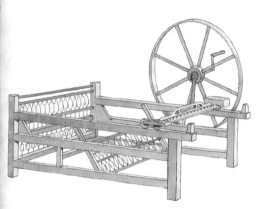

**1764** In England James Hargreaves invents the 'spinning jenny'. This mechanical spinning machine means one person can spin eight threads at a time, so increasing productivity. It replaces the spinning wheel.

**1770** French pharmacist Alexis Duchateau produces sets of false teeth made of hard mineral paste. Earlier false teeth were made of hippopotamus bone, but these turned brown and smelt awful.

*clack! clack!*

AAARGH!

*In 1783 the Montgolfier's balloon makes a flight and so becomes the first passenger-carrying 'aircraft'.*

**1788** American John Greenwood makes a dentist's drill using a spinning wheel. It is much better than the first dentist's drill made by the Roman surgeon Archigenes in the first century AD which was turned by a rope.

# Inventors

**Benjamin Franklin (1706-90)**
Benjamin Franklin had little formal education, yet he helped draw up the Declaration of Independence leading to the foundation of the United States of America. He proved that lightning was an electrical discharge by flying a kite in a storm, risking his own life in the process. From this discovery he developed the first lightning conductor.

**The Montgolfier Brothers**
**Joseph-Michael** (1740-1810) and **Jacques-Etienne** (1745-99) Montgolfier, the sons of a French paper manufacturer, made the first practical aircraft. They experimented with balloons, launching their first passengers – a cockerel, a duck and a sheep – in September 1783. The first manned flight came two months later.

**James Watt (1728-1819)**
Scottish engineer James Watt developed a much more efficient steam engine than Newcomen's engine, and it could also power a wheel. Steam could now be used to drive a whole range of machinery, and would be, literally, the driving force behind the big new factories of the Industrial Revolution.

# THE ELECTRIC REVOLUTION

Run a plastic comb through your hair and you may see sparks jump from the comb. They are caused by static electricity. Static electricity can also be produced by rubbing a cloth against glass – early generators worked like this. However, a better way to produce an electric current was discovered in 1800, when Italian scientist Alessandro Volta invented the battery. The battery produced a steady electric current. One scientist who experimented with the electric battery was the English scientist Michael Faraday. He invented the electric generator and the transformer.

## Events

**1799-1815** The Napoleonic Wars rage in Europe and beyond.

**1801** Italian astronomer Piazzi discovers the first asteroid – 'Ceres'.

**1804** Beethoven's Third Symphony, the 'Eroica', has its first performance.

**1811** A 12-year-old English girl, Mary Anning, discovers the fossil of an ichthyosaur.

**1815** Tambora, a volcano in Indonesia, erupts killing thousands. The dust it throws out causes temperatures to fall around the globe.

**1818** Mary Shelley writes *Frankenstein*. The 'creature' is brought to life with electricity.

## What's the big idea? ELECTRICITY

*Michael Faraday's 1832 generator produces a small electric current by moving a small copper needle near a magnet. A few months later Frenchman Hippolyte Pixii makes the first really practical generator and the modern electrical industry is born.*

# Inventions

**1800** Italian scientist Alessandro Volta invents the battery. The word 'voltage' comes from his name.

**1807** Robert Fulton builds the *Clermont*, the first passenger-carrying paddle steamer. For many years it steamed up and down the Hudson River between New York and Albany, in the USA.

**1815** English scientist Humphry Davy invents the safety lamp to prevent explosions in mines. The flame is inside a metal gauze shield so cannot ignite explosive gases in the mine.

**1816** Johann Maelzel invents the metronome, a device which indicates the exact tempo musicians should follow when playing a piece of music.

**1818** Building on the work of Frenchman Nicolas Appert in preserving food, an English company starts supplying canned food to the Royal Navy. But opening the can is still a hammer and chisel job – the tin-opener will not be invented until 1855.

*ted Veal*

**1823** Scotsman Charles Macintosh produces a waterproof cloth that he uses to make raincoats. The cloth is very smelly!

*niffy pong*

*Och, my coat's no that smelly.*

*oinky niff*

**1824** Blind since the age of three, Frenchman Louis Braille invents an alphabet for the blind. It uses a system of raised dots.

# Inventors

**Nicolas-Francois Appert (1752-1841)**
French confectioner who invented airtight containers for preserving food. He spent 14 years perfecting sealed glass jars in which fruits, vegetables, soups, dairy products and jams could be kept without going bad.

**Louis Braille (1809-52)**
Braille was blinded at the age of three when a knife he was using in his father's leather workshop slipped and stabbed him in the eye. The wound became infected and he lost the sight of both eyes. Seven years later he won a scholarship to the National Institute for Blind Youth in Paris. The system of raised dots, invented by Braille, was finally adopted as the written language of the blind in 1932, eighty years after his death. It is still used.

**Alessandro Volta (1745-1827)**
An Italian physicist, Volta found that contact between two different metals produces electricity. Using this knowledge he invented the first electric battery. It was called the 'voltaic pile' and consisted of pairs of silver and zinc discs between paper or cloth soaked in salt water. Volta's battery generated electricity from a chemical reaction in this pile of discs.

# TRAINS AND TRACKS

Railways are far older than locomotives. European mines had tracks for small horse-drawn wooden trucks in the fourteenth century. In 1803 Cornish engineer Richard Trevithick built the first locomotive. It was used at the Coalbrookdale Ironworks in Shropshire. Then, in 1812, mine inspector John Blenkinsop designed the first locomotives to work regularly. They were for a rack railway – the track had teeth which engaged with toothed wheels. George Stevenson, a mine engineer, built his first locomotive in 1814.

## What's the big idea? RAILWAYS

*Businessmen soon realised that fast services for passengers would be very profitable. In 1829 the Liverpool and Manchester Railway Company held trials at Rainhill, near Liverpool, to find the best engine. George Stevenson and his son Robert entered a new engine, the* Rocket. *Its boiler was an entirely new design: contact with 25 tubes heated from the firebox turned the water to steam. This feature and an improved exhaust system enabled the* Rocket *to pull a 14-tonne train at 47 kph – about twice as fast as its rivals.*

*Stevenson's* Rocket

## Events

**1819** In England it becomes illegal for children to work more than 12 hours a day.

**1819** The future Queen of England, Victoria is born. She died in 1901.

**1819** Albert, the future Prince Consort to Queen Victoria, is born. He died in 1861.

**1819** The USA buys the colony of Florida from Spain.

**1821** Population of countries (in millions): France 30.4; Germany 26.0; Great Britain 20.8; Italy 18.0; Austria 12.0; USA 9.6.

**1825** Introduction of horse-drawn buses in London.

**1829** Act of Parliament establishes the first police force in London.

# Inventions

**1829** French tailor Barthélemy makes the first sewing machine. He sets up a factory with 80 machines making army uniforms.

**1830** English textile worker Edwin Budding invents the first successful lawnmower. The mower was based on a cloth-cutting machine and today's cylinder mowers look very similar.

**1831** American Cyrus McCormick invents an efficient reaper to harvest grain crops. It is an improvement on the horse-drawn reaper invented in 1826 by Scottish minister Patrick Bell.

**1836** American gunsmith Samuel Colt starts mass-producing a simplified version of the revolver Elisha Collier and Artemis Wheeler invented in 1818.

**1840** In May the British post office introduces the first postage stamp, the Penny Black. Created by David Charles of Dundee, it has a picture of Queen Victoria's head.

*Penny Black*

Salariya Book Company Ltd
25 Marlborough Place
Brighton
East Sussex
BN1 1UB

# Inventors

### Joseph Nicéphore Niepce (1765-1833)

The Frenchman Joseph Niepce used a pinhole camera to take the first photograph. At the back of the camera was a metal plate coated with bitumen. After eight hours the bitumen had hardened where the light was strongest. When the soft bitumen was washed off an image remained.

### Charles Babbage (1752-1841)

As a young man the English mathematician Charles Babbage made barrel organs. These pushed air through holes punched in cards and into each pipe at exactly the right moment to play the tune. Using the same method he made a machine to make mathematical calculations instead of musical notes. This 'Analytical Engine' was the very first digital computer.

### Lady Augusta Ada Byron Lovelace (1815-1851)

Daughter of the English poet Lord Byron, Ada is really the first computer programmer. In 1834 she met Sir Charles Babbage (above). A brilliant mathematician herself, she wrote a 'code' for how Babbage's machine could calculate numbers. This is now seen as the first 'computer programme'.

# FACTORIES AND TOOLS

In the first half of the nineteenth century Britain became 'the workshop of the world'. New tools enabled British engineers to build all types of advanced machinery. With a well-developed iron industry to supply materials and steam engines for power, many new inventions were exported. A transport revolution in rail, shipping and civil engineering made the world seem much smaller. Machine tools played an important part in technical progress. Screws, rods and cylinders could be made of a size and accuracy that had been impossible before. Skilled craftsmen were replaced by machinery, and goods could be mass-produced for the first time.

## Events

**1833** Britain takes possession of the Falkland Islands off the coast of Argentina.

**1836** American rebels are massacred by Mexican forces at the Alamo mission station. Texas separates from Mexico and forms a republic.

**1843** American Samuel Morse invents a new telegraph code.

**1845** The Irish Famine begins.

**1848** Germans Karl Marx and Friedrich Engels publish the *Communist Manifesto*.

**1853** Englishman George Cayley builds the first glider to be flown by a pilot over 450 metres (above).

**1859** Englishman Charles Darwin publishes his theory of human evolution.

**1859** The discovery of oil in the USA leads to the birth of the modern oil industry.

## What's the big idea? EXPLOSIVES

**BOOM!**

*When nitric acid and glycerine are mixed together they form a yellow liquid called nitroglycerine. This liquid is a very unstable but extremely powerful explosive.*

*Alfred Nobel combined nitroglycerine with an absorbent material to form a solid, powerful explosive that was much safer to use. In 1867 Nobel patented this material as dynamite.*

# Inventions

**1837** First use of the electric telegraph developed by William Cooke and Charles Wheatstone. Swinging needles transmit messages in code.

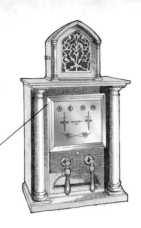

*The first electric telegraph*

*Daguerrotype process camera*

**1839** The Daguerrotype process camera is invented by Louis Daguerre. It weighs about 50 kg and uses poisonous mercury vapours in the developing process.

**1840s** African-American Benjamin Bradley invents a steam engine for a warship. Unable to get a patent, Bradley sells his invention to buy his freedom from a life of slavery.

**1846** African-American Norbert Rillieux patents his invention of the sugar-refining evaporator. It is still used in the sugar industry.

**1849** Claude Minie invents the Minie ball (right), a bullet for guns with grooved bores (such as rifles). When fired, the bullet expands to clean out the grooves of the bore. European and American armies adopt Minie's bullet.

**1851** Isaac Singer patents his lock-stitch sewing machine, which works by treading a pedal ('treadle'). A toothed wheel moves the fabric on between stitches and a presser foot holds the fabric in place.

# Inventors

**Alfred Nobel (1833-96)**
Swedish chemist Alfred Nobel discovered how to use nitroglycerine, a highly explosive substance, so it would not explode unless used with a detonator. He called his invention dynamite and it was the first safe explosive. It made Nobel rich and he gave £2 million to set up the Nobel Prizes, which are awarded each year for achievements in peace, physics, chemistry, literature and medicine.

**Henry Bessemer (1813-98)**
The English engineer Henry Bessemer made his first fortune selling 'gold' powder made from brass as a paint additive. Although he also invented successful devices for glass-making, textiles and sugar-processing methods, he is best known for his invention of the Bessemer process, the first successful method of mass-producing steel cheaply (page 39).

# BRIGHT LIGHTS, BIG CITIES

**M**any of the things we take for granted today were introduced during the nineteenth century, without them towns and cities could not have grown so quickly. One of the most important developments was a safe supply of water. In many towns clean drinking water was piped into homes. Sewage systems were built, and electricity and gas supplies developed. Railways grew rapidly, making the transport of people and goods cheaper and easier.

*Outbreaks of cholera were common in European towns and cities. In 1854 the cause is discovered: polluted water. Governments begin building water and sewage systems in the growing cities. London's main drainage system is a network of five main sewers running across the city, linked by four large pumping stations.*

What's the **big** idea?

## URBAN LIFE

*In the late 1880s electric trams are introduced in America, Britain and Germany.*

*Gradually, modern conveniences, like gas or electric lighting, hot and cold running water and flush toilets, begin to appear in the homes of the wealthy in towns and cities.*

# Inventions

**1852** Frenchman Henri Giffard makes the first flight in his streamlined hydrogen-filled airship. A steam engine turns the propeller to drive it along. It takes its inventor 27 km from Paris to Trappes.

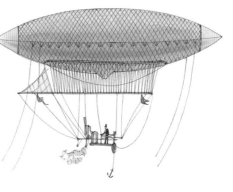

**1856** Henry Bessemer designs a converter to blow air through molten iron to turn it into steel. Although no longer used, it was an extremely important invention at the time.

**1857** Joseph Gayetty invents the first toilet paper composed of flat sheets of paper.

**1866** The first undersea cable is laid between Britain and America.

# Events

rattle rattle squeak!

**1861** Frenchman Ernest Michaux invents the 'Boneshaker', a bicycle with pedals on the front wheel.

**1863** The world's first underground railway station is built in London.

**1864** The Red Cross Society is founded in Geneva to care for war casualties.

**1865** French scientist Louis Pasteur publishes his germ theory of disease.

**1868** English convicts are sent to Australia to work in prison colonies.

**1870** Rome becomes the capital of newly united Italy.

**1876** At the Battle of Little Big Horn, the US army is defeated by Cheyenne and Sioux warriors.

**1879** Britain and France control Egypt.

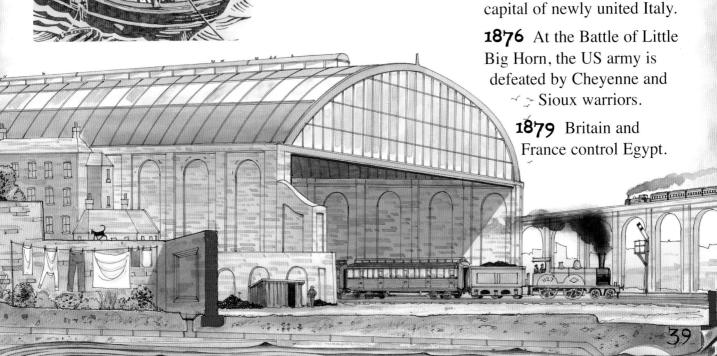

# NEW COMMUNICATIONS

**B**y the end of the nineteenth century electricity had revolutionised communications. In 1800 most messages were transported by riders on horseback, in horse-drawn vehicles or by ship. By 1900 electric telegraphs could send messages across continents in a few hours, telephone systems were common in Europe and America and the first radio systems were being developed. Radio communication as we know it grew out of the discoveries made in the nineteenth century by scientists like the Italian Guglielmo Marconi.

## What's the big idea?
## THE LIGHT BULB

*In 1878 both the American Thomas Edison (far right) and the Englishman Joseph Swan make light bulbs. They exhibit them at the Great Electrical Exhibition in Paris in 1881, where they receive wide publicity. Soon their light bulbs are used in all electric light fittings.*

*Thomas Edison*

## Events

**1880** The first Anglo-Boer War between Britain and the Afrikaners in South Africa begins.

**1881** Czar Alexander II of Russia is assassinated.

**1884** In Britain, the Reform Act gives the vote to all men over the age of 21.

**1886** After years of unrest in Ireland, the British government introduces a bill for Home Rule. It is defeated.

**1887** France establishes an Indo-Chinese Union.

**1889** The Eiffel Tower is built in Paris.

**1890** At the Battle of Wounded Knee, the Sioux people are defeated and disarmed. It is the last Native American uprising.

**1890s** The Art Nouveau style is popular in Europe.

**1892** Russia begins a period of modernisation and industrial development, and enters an alliance with France in the following year.

# Inventions

*transmitter*

**1876** The telephone is invented by Alexander Graham Bell. It has a transmitter (left) that sends the sounds and a receiver (below) which receives them. Connected by a wire, each part has a 'reed'– a thin piece of metal – near an electric magnet. The reed vibrates whenever someone speaks near the transmitter. Then the magnet vibrates, sending an electric current to the receiver. The current causes the reed in the receiver to move, which reproduces the words spoken into the transmitter.

*receiver*

**1880s** Telephones develop rapidly, with networks springing up in towns. Telephone exchanges connect subscribers. The first automatic exchange is invented in 1889, the same year that coin-operated phones are developed.

**1885** The first petrol car is built by a German engineer, Karl Benz. A three-wheeled vehicle, it is powered by a one-cylinder gasoline engine.

*engine*

**1891** Edison invents the kinetoscope – a slot machine that shows a 15-second film. A mechanism turns the film reel while the picture is viewed through a peephole at the top.

*reel mechanism*

*peephole*

**1891** German engineer Otto Lilienthal experiments with monoplanes and biplane gliders. In 1896 he will be killed in a crash, unable to fulfil his dream of a powered-flight machine.

# Inventors

### Thomas Edison (1847-1931)

Edison's inventions have a great influence on twentieth-century life. His first invention was a repeating telegraph and telegraphic printer. Although his most famous invention was the light bulb, Edison also created the kinetoscope – the first film projector for moving pictures or 'movies'.

### Guglielmo Marconi (1874-1937)

Marconi, an Italian physicist and electrical engineer, invented radio and wireless communication. By using electromagnetic waves, he transmitted messages, and in 1895 achieved the first radio link. In 1901 he sent the first cross-Atlantic radio signal.

### Lewis Latimer (1848-1929)

African-American Latimer (above) designed inexpensive electric lighting. He set up electric lighting in New York, Philadelphia and London. His book, *Incandescent Electric Lighting,* became the essential textbook for lighting engineers. Latimer also did the drawings in Alexander Graham Bell's patent application for the telephone.

41

# LEARNING TO FLY

huff! puff!

The first successful flying machines were hot-air balloons, like the Montgolfier brothers' balloon (page 31). However it was the turn of the century – the end of the nineteeth and the beginning of the twentieth centuries – when powered flight literally took off. It would continue throughout the twentieth century, with supersonic passenger planes, manned missions to the moon and unmanned flights to planets such as Mars. But the development of the internal combustion engine and the motor car in these years would have more effect on people's lives than travel to the moon.

What's the **big** idea?

# MAN-POWERED FLIGHT

## Events

**1893** Women in New Zealand become the first in the world to get the vote.

**1895** Austrian psychiatrist Sigmund Freud publishes his first work on psychoanalysis.

**1896** In South Africa the British try to take over the Transvaal but the Boers defeat them.

**1898** French scientists, Pierre and Marie Curie, announce the discovery of radium. It made the first radiotherapy treatments for cancer possible.

WE DID IT!

# Inventions

**1900S** Safe blood transfusions are possible after Karl Landsteiner discovers people have different blood types so need blood matching their own – many earlier transfusions had killed the patient. He identifies blood groups A, B, AB and O.

*You'll be fine now that we know your blood type.*

**1900** A patent is granted for a dust cleaner that sucks air through a nozzle – the future vacuum cleaner.

**1900** In Germany Count Ferdinand von Zeppelin, builds the first rigid airship or 'zeppelin' (left).

**1900** The first modern submarine (right) is launched in America. Many earlier attempts had all been unsuccessful.

**1900** Electric kettles become available. Few homes have electricity, but inventors realise that when they do it will make daily living much easier.

**1901** American travelling salesman, King Camp Gillette invents the safety razor with disposable double-edged blades. He wanted to invent something that would be used once, thrown away and replaced by a new one. By 1906 90,000 razors and 12,400,000 blades had been sold.

# Inventors

## THE WRIGHT BROTHERS

Orville (left) and Wilbur Wright (right) grew up in Dayton, Ohio, America. As boys, their father gave them a toy helicopter, sparking a life-long interest in flying. When they grew up, the brothers ran a bicycle-making business, but never stopped thinking about the problems of flight.

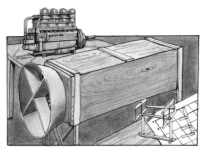

The brothers designed and made wings, testing them in a wind tunnel to find which design produced the most lift and was best in flight. They made a light but powerful petrol engine and built an efficient propeller system, discovering that for the maximum forward thrust the propeller should turn more slowly than the engine. On 17th December, 1903 Orville kept their plane, *Flyer*, in the air for 12 seconds – the first flight. They went on making planes until Wibur died of typhoid fever in 1912. Orville died in 1948.

# MASS PRODUCTION

The First World War broke out in 1914. Its effect on technological developments was dramatic. Machine guns, poison gas and tanks meant battles had to be fought in new ways. Aircraft became deadly weapons and submarines threatened shipping.

In America, Henry Ford made motoring affordable for most people by using mass-production techniques to make cars cheaply. With a top speed of 65 kph, *Model T*s rolled off the production line every 90 seconds. In 1908, a *Model T* cost US$850 (about one year's salary for a manual worker). When the *Model T* went out of production in 1927, more than 15 million cars had been made.

## What's the big idea? MASS-PRODUCED CARS

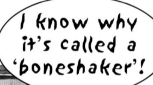

I know why it's called a 'boneshaker'!

## Events

**1901** Queen Victoria dies; Edward VII becomes king of Great Britain.

**1905** German scientist Albert Einstein publishes his Theory of Relativity.

**1909** Louis Blériot of France flies across the English Channel in a tiny monoplane which was seldom more than a metre above the sea.

**1910** Revolution in Mexico is followed by dictatorships and social disorder.

**1911** Ernest Rutherford, a physicist from New Zealand, shows that atoms have a nucleus.

**1912** Roald Amundsen of Norway is the first person to reach the South Pole.

**1912** In China the Manchu dynasty is overthrown. It is replaced by a republic, but the country becomes unstable as warlords fight for power.

# Inventions

**1902** The Teddy Bear is created by Morris Michtom. President Theodore Roosevelt had refused to shoot a bear on a trip to Louisiana, so the toy is called 'Teddy's bear'.

**1907** Frenchman Paul Cornu builds a twin-rotor helicopter and makes a brief flight, but unfortunately did not have the money to continue his experiments. It would not be until the 1930s that the first stable and usable helicopter was made.

**1909** The first electric toaster is produced by the General Electric Company in New York. More electric appliances are invented soon after, among them hand-held hairdryers (1920), refrigerators (1923) and razors (1928).

**1910** Henri Fabre builds his *Hydravion*. This strange-looking seaplane flies tail first and has no fuselage (body) to sit in. Instead, the pilot perches on two wooden girders. In place of wheels, the craft has three floats.

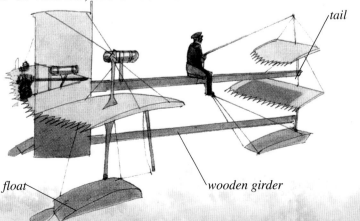

*float*

*tail*

*wooden girder*

# Inventors

### Henry Ford (1863-1947)

American industrial pioneer, Henry Ford built his first car in 1896. In 1908 he introduced his famous *Model T* – a car that was easy to make and repair. The car was easy to drive, too. It had a two-speed gearbox that worked with a single pedal. But the real secret of Ford's success was the mass-production methods he used in his factories (below). This made his cars much cheaper, so more people could afford them.

### George W. Carver (1865-1943)

African-American George Carver was an agricultural chemist and a highly successful inventor. He invented hundreds of uses for peanuts and soybeans. Carver also invented adhesives, bleach, fuel briquettes, ink, instant coffee, linoleum, metal polish, shaving cream, shoe polish and wood stain!

45

# THE BROADCASTING AGE

Radio and television carry messages on electromagnetic waves that were discovered by the German physicist Heinrich Hertz in 1887. In 1901 Guglielmo Marconi sent a radio signal from England to Canada, so proving that radio waves can carry messages over very long distances. In 1925 John Logie Baird from Scotland transmitted the first television pictures. Then in 1929 he persuaded the British Broadcasting Corporation (BBC) to transmit the world's first television service. It was received by all the televisions in the world – all 100 of them! In 1937, the BBC adopted an all-electronic broadcasting system. This gave better pictures, was more reliable, used more mobile cameras and was cheaper than Baird's system.

## What's the big idea?
## TELEVISION

*In 1926 John Logie Baird gives the first public demonstration of his television system by transmitting a small and blurred picture of a ventriloquist's dummy.*

Now I just need to sort this wire out and we'll have a perfect picture!

## Events

**1912**  The *Titanic*, built to be unsinkable, hits an iceberg on its maiden voyage and sinks. Over 1500 people drown.

**1914**  The Panama Canal linking the Atlantic and Pacific oceans opens.

**1914**  The murder of Archduke Franz Ferdinand in Sarajevo leads to the start of the First World War.

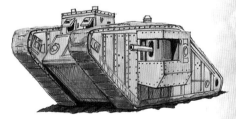

**1916**  Tanks are developed as a way to cross trenches, crush barbed-wire barricades and destroy gun positions. Early tanks are slow and unreliable.

**1916**  The Battle of the Somme: 624,000 Allied and up to 680,000 German soldiers die. Tanks are used in battle for the first time.

**1917**  As the First World War grinds on, army commanders begin to use tanks in large numbers in battle.

# Inventions

**FRITZ HABER**

**1914** Fritz Haber, the German scientist who discovered how to make ammonia (important for making artificial fertilisers), advises the German government how to make explosives with it. He helps organise gas attacks, as well as defences against them.

**1920** The first hand-held hairdryer is made by the Racine Universal Motor Company in the USA. A small electric motor blows air over a heated filament.

**1923** The Sterling "Threeflex" valve radio receiver (right) is invented. Its aerial can be rotated to pick up the best signal.

**1926** Robert Goddard launches the first successful liquid-fuel rocket (left). It is the forerunner of Germany's V-2 missile and later space launch vehicles.

**1925** The Belinographe telephoto machine (below) is used to transmit black-and-white pictures through the telephone network. It is the precursor of modern facsimile (fax) machines.

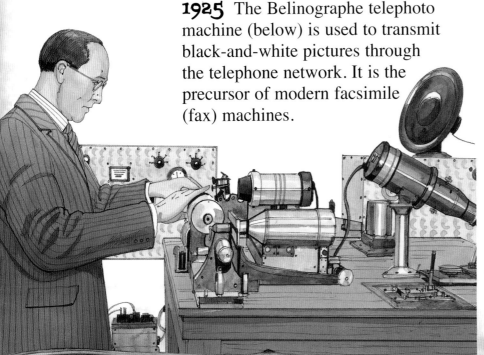

# Television

*Above* The first televised images on Baird's equipment looked something like this.

Television has become the world's favourite form of entertainment, bringing action into our homes at the touch of a button. Britain started the first black-and-white public service through the BBC in 1936 when a TV set cost around £125 – a very large sum then. Television spread throughout Europe after the Second World War, while colour TV developed in the US during the late 1940s. Today we have advanced technology like digital TV and DVD players.

*Below* A 1935 television set showing the cathode ray tube, the radio receiver and the loudspeaker.

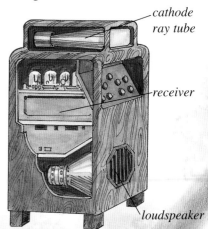

cathode ray tube

receiver

loudspeaker

# SOPHISTICATED WEAPONS

The Second World War broke out in September 1939 and the inventions that sprang from it changed the lives of everyone. New weapons of mass destruction appeared, including the German V-2, which was the first long-range rocket missile, and the first atomic bombs – dropped on Japan in 1945.

The new, highly sophisticated weapons being developed needed equally sophisticated systems to control them. This led to the development of the first electronic computers – the forerunners of those we use today – and was the beginning of an enormous new international industry.

## What's the big idea? THE JET ENGINE

*The jet engine is developed simultaneously by Frank Whittle in Britain and by Hans von Ohain in Germany. But it is the Germans who build and fly the first jet aircraft – in August 1939. Jet engines can be much more powerful than piston engines.*

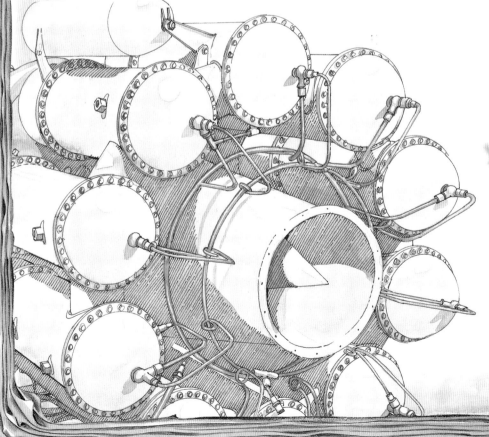

## Events

**1923** Russia is renamed the Union of Soviet Socialist Republics (USSR) after the 1917 October Revolution and the royal family's execution.

**1927** American astronomer Edwin Hubble discovers there are many galaxies in space.

**1930** Englishwoman Amy Johnson is the first woman to fly solo from London to Darwin, Australia.

**1935** The Nuremberg Laws in Germany begin persecution of the Jews living there.

**1936** Jesse Owens, the African-American athlete, wins four gold medals at the Olympic Games, Nuremburg. Hitler is outraged.

**1939** Germany invades Poland and the Second World War begins.

**1940** With fewer than 1000 Hurricanes and Spitfires (above), the RAF defeats the Luftwaffe (German Air Force) which had more than 3000 aircraft.

# Inventions

**1930** The *Kavor* hydraulically powered toothbrush is invented. It is attached to the tap with a tube and the water pressure swivels the brush.

**1933** Carlton Magee invents the parking meter. The 1938 version is shown right.

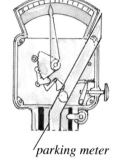

**1938** Chester Carlson invents photocopying. His prototype photocopier is shown on the right.

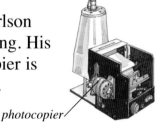

*photocopier*

*parking meter*

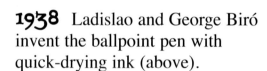

**1938** Ladislao and George Biró invent the ballpoint pen with quick-drying ink (above).

**1939** Britain builds radar defences around the coast against German attack. Radar (**ra**dio **d**etection **a**nd **r**anging) uses radio waves to detect objects and measure their distances. It works in all weather and at night.

*Radar is an important part of a country's defence system.*

*The first computers are enormous, and they make a big difference in the time it takes to make mathematical calculations.*

**1946** The ENIAC (Electronic Numerical Integrator and Computer) is the first modern electronic computer. It takes up a large room and weighs 30 tonnes. It carries out in an hour calculations that had previously taken a year.

Wow! This machine is so fast!

# Inventors

## Alexander Fleming (1881-1955)

Alexander Fleming was a Scottish scientist who specialised in the study of bacteria. In 1928, quite by chance, he noticed that a mould on one of his dishes of bacteria was killing the germs around it. This mould belonged to a group of spores called Penicillium.

Working on this observation, the scientists Howard Florey and Ernest Chain discovered how to turn the penicillium spores into one of the most important tools of modern medicine. Penicillin was first given to a patient in 1940 and has helped reduce death from septic infections ever since.

*Penicillin mould surrounded by bacteria*

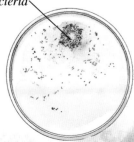

# GLOBAL SUPERPOWERS

After the end of the Second World War in 1945 technology developed increasingly fast as the world entered the Space Age. The world's two superpowers, the USSR and the United States, competed fiercely against each other to be first in space. The USSR launched the first artificial satellite in 1957, proving to the Americans it was a powerful military state.

The two countries also competed in the field of nuclear power, not only as a source of energy, but also for nuclear weapons. Both the United States and the USSR developed the hydrogen bomb – a bomb even more destructive than the atom bomb.

## What's the big idea? NUCLEAR ENERGY

I hope I don't end up glowing in the dark!

*In 1956 Britain's first nuclear power station, Calder Hall, opened. Power stations like these not only offered a cheap source of electricity, but could also produce plutonium for nuclear weapons.*

## Events

**1941** Japan attacks the US naval base at Pearl Harbor and the US enters the Second World War.

**1945** The US drops atom bombs on Japan. Germany and Japan surrender. The Second World War ends. Nazi leaders are tried for their crimes at Nuremburg. The Nazis killed some six million Jews and other races during the Second World War.

**1945** The United Nations (UN) is established.

**1949** North Atlantic Treaty Organisation (NATO) formed to counter the threat of the Communist USSR.

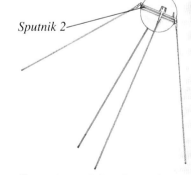

*Sputnik 2*

**1957** The USSR launches its first artificial satellite, Sputnik 1. Sputnik 2 (above), with Laika the dog on board, follows later in the year.

**1958** Chinese Communist leader Mao Zedong unveils the Great Leap Forward plan for industrial growth.

# Inventions

**1947** The transistor (left) is invented. Using electricity to control electricity, it is the start of modern electronics.

**1953** Joseph Salk finds a vaccine to prevent polio. People suffering from the disease were treated in an iron lung – an artificial respirator.

**1954** Nuclear-powered ships and submarines are built. The US and the USSR make the first hydrogen bombs.

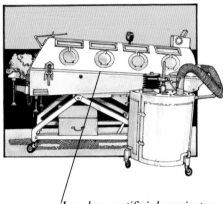

*Iron lung artificial respirator*

**1955** Narinder Kapany invents optical fibres. They can carry light around curves and in the 1970s will lead to dramatic improvements in communications.

**1955** Christopher Cockerell invents the hovercraft. The first full-sized one is tested in May 1959. Large car-carrying hovercraft will be developed in the 1960s and operate across the English Channel.

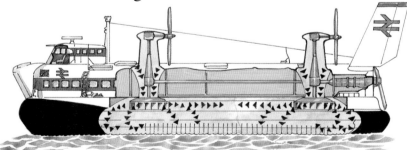

**1956** The oral contraceptive pill is developed.

**1957** The USSR's R-7 missile launches the Sputnik satellites. The size and power of the R-7 proves it could be used to fire nuclear weapons across the Atlantic.

*Russian R-7 missile*

**J. Robert Oppenheimer (1904-67)**
The American physicist Robert Oppenheimer developed the atomic bomb in his laboratory in New Mexico. In 1945, having spent $2,000 million, he tested his project for the first time. Scientists looked on in awe at the vast atomic cloud that mushroomed 37,000 m into the sky.

**Francis Crick (1916-2004)**
In 1962 Francis Crick from England and American James Watson received the Nobel Prize for their discovery of the double helix structure of DNA – the genetic material in all living organisms. Their discovery was the beginning of molecular biology, from which developed techniques like genetic therapy and cloning.

**James Watson (born 1928)**

51

# THE RACE FOR SPACE

On 12th April, 1961 the USSR became the first country to put a man in space. In 1969 US astronaut Neil Armstrong was the first man to set foot on the moon. Since the 1960s satellites have been used to observe the weather, spy on other countries and provide communication links. This global communications satellite system means that news from anywhere in the world can instantly reach TV screens everywhere. The introduction of integrated circuits led to computers becoming smaller and cheaper because many transistors could be etched on a single sliver of silicone.

Public concern about nuclear power and pollution grew and, together with greater environmental awareness, result in the passing of laws to stop some of the worst pollution.

## Events

*"We choose to go to the moon in this decade..."*

**1961** US President Kennedy vows that America will put a man on the moon and bring him safely back before 1970.

**1963** Russian Valentina Tereshkova is the first woman in space.

**1963** The USSR, UK and USA all agree to ban nuclear tests.

**1965** US astronaut Edward White is the first American to walk in space.

**1969** American astronauts land on the moon. Millions watch on television as Neil Armstrong takes his first step.

What's the **big** idea?

## MAN ON THE MOON

No cheese here, NASA.

# Inventions

**1960** Theodore Maiman builds the first laser. It produces a thin, powerful beam of light. Lasers are now used in many fields, including communications and surgery.

*laser*

**1961** The USSR launches the first manned flight into space. Major Yuri Gagarin becomes the first man in space and makes a single orbit of Earth before landing near the River Volga in Russia.

**1962** Telstar (left) is launched. It is the the world's first international communications satellite and can carry long-distance TV broadcasts.

**1962** The first computer game is created. It is called 'Spacewar'.

**1963** Research engineers make strong and durable carbon fibre by applying controlled levels of heat to synthetic fibres.

**1964** American firm IBM inserts into an electric typewriter a device in which text, with layout details, can be stored electronically on magnetic tape as it is typed. In this way, large quantities of text can be stored on tape.

**1967** The skateboard is created by surfers, who nail the bases of roller skates to the undersides of wooden planks. People can now 'surf' without the sea.

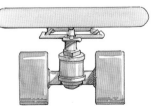

**1967** The first successful human heart transplant is performed. During the operation, the donor's heart is attached to the top half of the recipient's heart, after which all the air is removed and the final stitching is completed.

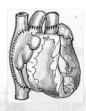

**Wernher von Braun (1912-77)**
Von Braun was the German scientist who developed the V-2 missile during the Second World War. After Germany's defeat in 1945, von Braun surrendered to the US and became an American citizen. In the USA he was a leading scientist in the space programme.

**Sergei Korolev (1907-66)**
Korolev was the scientist behind the Soviet space programme. He and his colleague Valentin Glushko were the engineers responsible for Sputnik 1, the first artificial satellite, launched on 4th October, 1957.

**Dr Christiaan Barnard (1922-2001)**
South African Barnard performed the first successful human heart transplant. The patient's body rejected the organ, he died after 14 days, but nowadays 75% of patients survive surgery.

# MODERN TECHNOLOGY

Modern computers use silicon chips or integrated circuits instead of the valves which drove the first mechanical and electronic computers. All the components and connections necessary for an electrical circuit can be put on a piece of silicon the size of a child's fingernail. The chips are then placed in a box with legs, to which the electrical wiring of the computer hardware is attached. In 1971 American engineers Federico Faggin, Ted Hoff and Stan Mazor invented the microprocessor, a chip that had all the main parts of a computer on a single piece of silicon. This would become the 'brain' of the personal computer. In 1977 the first successful personal computer, the Apple II, was launched in the USA. Since then computers have become part of everyday life.

## What's the big idea?

## PERSONAL COMPUTERS

Help! Where's my file?!

## Events

**1970** After a military coup, Idi Amin seizes power in Uganda.

**1972** Pakistan is forced to give up East Pakistan, which becomes Bangladesh.

**1973** The Yom Kippur War between Israel and the Arab states leads to oil restrictions, sending oil prices soaring and causing a global economic crisis.

**1973** The Sydney Opera House opens, having taken 14 years to build.

**1974** The tomb of Chinese emperor Qin Shi Huangdi is discovered. It holds 7500 pottery figures and artefacts.

**1976** Concorde, the first supersonic passenger plane, starts transatlantic flights.

**1976** Many countries adopt the Helsinki Convention on Human Rights.

**1979** Margaret Thatcher becomes the UK's first woman prime minister.

**1979** Civil war against the pro-Soviet regime breaks out in Afghanistan. The USSR sends troops to defend the government.

# Inventions

**1971** The microprocessor appears. It holds the 'central processing unit' (CPU) of a computer compressed into a tiny chip of silicon.

**1971** The first space station, the Soviets' Salyut-1, is launched. All the crew die when their capsule loses air on its return to earth.

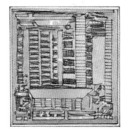

**1972** The first CAT scanner is produced. CAT (Computerised Axial Tomography) X-rays three-dimensional sections through the body. With it, doctors can tell if a tumour is present and also roughly how deep it is in the body. CAT scans give more information than an ordinary X-ray.

**1972** The availability of cheap, miniature computer devices leads to many new products, like video games (below right) and pocket calculators.

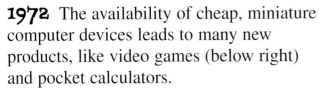

**1978** The first test-tube baby is born. Human egg cells are fertilised in a dish until they form a pre-embryo. This is then implanted into the mother's womb.

**1978** The popular *Space Invaders* video game (right) follows the success of *PONG* (far right) – the first commercial video game, released in 1972.

**1979** The Sony Walkman is the first personal stereo on the market. A small tape cassette player with light headphones, it gives people the chance to listen to music while on the move.

# Inventors

### Steven Jobs
### (born 1955)
American Steven Jobs co-founded Apple Computers to mass-produce personal computers. Jobs and his friend Steven Wozniak designed computer games for Atari before they started Apple in the 1970s. Jobs also started the NeXT software company and Pixar animation studios.

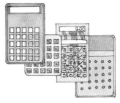

### Stephen Wozniak
### (born 1951)
American Stephen Wozniak used a cheap microprocessor and several memory chips to build a computer that was better than others of the 1970s. He called it Apple I. He and Steven Jobs formed the Apple Computer Corporation and became multimillionaires.

### Bill Gates
### (born 1955)
As a student, Gates saw the home computer market growing and realised the need for software. After he sold the rights to a programme he'd written, Gates left Harvard and formed Microsoft.

# THE FINAL FRONTIER

The American space shuttle made its first flight in 1981. But in 1986 public confidence in complicated technologies was shattered by two dramatic accidents. The American space shuttle *Challenger* exploded soon after launch on 28th January. Then, on 25th April, a nuclear reactor at Chernobyl in the USSR blew up. The effects of the radioactivity that the explosion spread over Europe can still be felt. Nuclear power programmes in other countries were scaled down or stopped.

The European Space Agency's *Spacelab* laboratory was launched in 1983. It was expensive and scientists thought unmanned satellites better value. The US stopped its manned space programme until 1988.

## What's the big idea?
## SPACE SHUTTLES

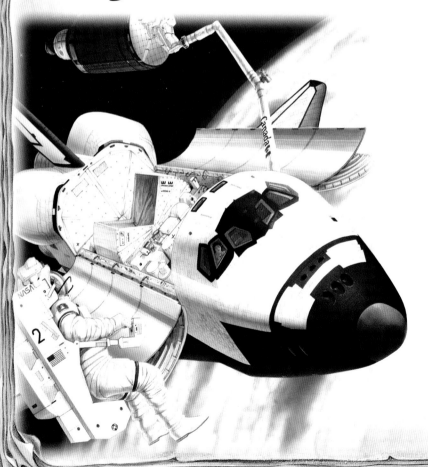

## Events

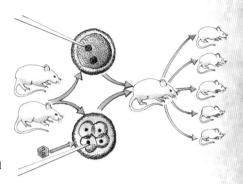

**1981** In America, the first transgenetic animals are produced. They are created by removing a fertilised egg, injecting DNA from another species, and then replacing the egg. The first transgenetic animals (mice) were given a growth gene and grew up to 50% larger than normal mice.

**1980s** Word-processing programmes become available and personal computers replace type-writers. PCs (above) are also used for video games.

**1980s** In Germany, magnetic levitation (maglev) trains are developed to provide a high-speed form of transportation.

# Inventions

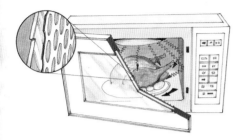

**1970S** Microwave ovens use a beam of high-energy radio waves to cook food.

**1980S** Portable phones become a common sight. People see them as symbols of status and wealth.

**1980** The first compact discs (above) are produced. They do not scratch like vinyl records.

**1980S** Cheap computing power is used in manufacturing as robotic production lines become more common. Robots are used to weld car bodies and spray them with paint (left). More versatile robots can perform simple assembly tasks. Modern production lines have robots that are each programmed for a different job.

Facsimile (fax) machines now use microprocessors, but they cannot be widely used until international standards make different brands compatible.

**1985** Camcorders (video cameras/recorders) become more popular after the smaller and lighter Video 8 system is introduced.

**1987** The introduction of digital audio tape recorders improves the quality of sound recording.

# Inventors

### Gertrude Elion (1918-99)

American Gertrude Elion's research changed medicine and drug-manufacturing. In 1954 she patented a drug for leukaemia that now helps 80% of children survive the disease. She also created a drug that helps the body accept transplanted organs. In 1983 Elion developed the world's first anti-viral drug. This laid the foundation for AZT, which is a vital drug in the treatment of AIDS. As a woman in a male-dominated field, Elion spent decades in junior positions before getting a research post. In 1988 she shared the Nobel Prize in Medicine with her colleague, George Hitchings.

### Patricia Bath (born 1942)

In 1988 opthalmologist Dr Patricia Bath became the first African-American woman to patent a medical invention – a laser device to vaporise cataracts quickly and painlessly. Bath's invention transformed eye surgery and made cataract treatment much more accurate. Together with her later inventions, Bath has helped to restore sight to people who have been blind for over 30 years.

57

# LIVING IN A CYBERWORLD

**W**ant to see how much the world has changed? Log on to the Internet, launch a search engine, type in any word and you'll get thousands of results. You can find out about anything online – news, shopping, entertainment and travel – literally any subject you can think of. Millions of interconnected threads in the Internet have become the mass medium for the twenty-first century. With e-mail and Internet access, you can be anywhere on the planet without being held back by time, space or long-distance phone tariffs.

## What's the big idea? WORLD WIDE WEB

*The World Wide Web is held together by HTTP (**h**ypertext **t**ransfer **p**rotocol), a code that links all electronic files across the Internet. This allows you to jump easily between web pages. Every page has a unique location or web address, also called a URL – **u**niversal **r**esource **l**ocator. Web pages are written in a computer language called HTML (**h**ypertext **m**arkup **l**anguage), which links your computer to other pages. You view the Web by using browser software. Type in a web address and the browser brings the web page to your screen from the web server that hosts the site.*

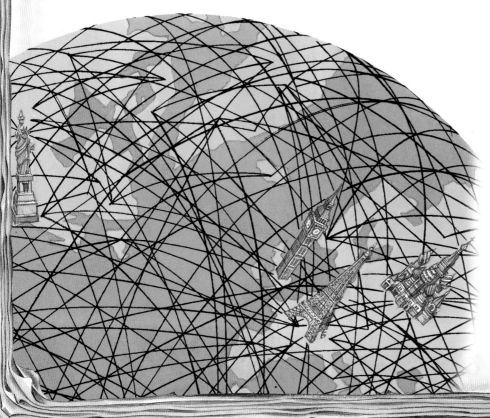

## Events

**1990** Germany is reunified.

**1991** Civil war breaks out in Yugoslavia.

**1991** The World Wide Web makes its official debut. Within five years the number of Internet users will jump from 600,000 to 40 million.

**1992** The first UN summit on the environment is held in Rio de Janeiro, Brazil.

**1993** The Native Titles Bill in passed in Australia to try to restore land rights to the native Aboriginals.

**1994** The underwater Channel Tunnel between Britain and France opens.

**1994** After 27 years in prison, Nelson Mandela is elected as President of South Africa following the first multiracial elections.

**1995** A massive earthquake causes major destruction in Kobe, Japan.

**1995** At an EU summit in Madrid a single European currency, the Euro, is planned for 1999.

**1997** Diana, Princess of Wales, is killed in a car crash in Paris.

# Inventions

**1991** Virtual reality arcade games are introduced. Video helmets take players to a world of sound and pictures that seems like real life.

Concern about the environment grows. Catalytic converters are put into cars so that harmful lead need not be put in petrol.

*catalytic converter in a car*

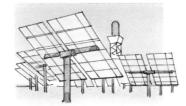

*printout of a person's unique DNA pattern*

DNA fingerprinting, developed in the 1980s, converts a DNA sample into a pattern that is unique for every human.

Solar power stations (right) can collect enough energy to supply a small town. This is a possible alternative to fossil fuels.

Wind power can generate electricity without pollution, but wind farms (left) need to be large to produce enough energy.

Energy from waves is another alternative power source to coal and oil. The waves' movement drives generators in the barges (right) to create energy.

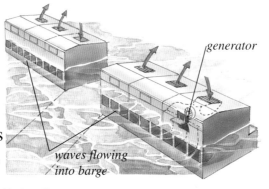

*generator*

*waves flowing into barge*

Is this the future of medicine? Nanorobots (right) will have tiny tools for microsurgery. They can pump drugs to, or remove toxins from, the body's cells. A minute communication dish in the patient's body will relay data to and from doctors.

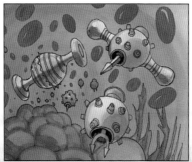

# Inventors

## Krisztina Holly (born 1968)

American Krisztina Holly developed the world's first computer-generated full-colour reflection hologram. She also co-developed a head-eye vision robot and a robotic tracking programme for the main engines of space shuttles. In 1992 she invented a commercial barcode scanner. Holly also invented the first Windows-based computer telephony software for call-answering and call-placing, voice mail and fax transmission.

## Tim Berners-Lee (born 1955)

Tim Berners-Lee turned a powerful communications system into a mass medium. Despite the growth and success of the World Wide Web, American Berners-Lee has always chosen the non-profit road. He has fought to keep the Web open and free to all users. Many of his colleagues are Internet millionaires; Berners-Lee works as the director of the W3 Consortium, a body that helps software companies agree on openly published protocols, instead of stalling one another's progress by withholding new technology.

# THE NEW MILLENIUM

As the twenty-first century dawned, mankind's technological progress was astonishing. In 2000, US and Russian cosmonauts became the first full-time tenants of the International Space Station orbiting 384 km above Kazakhstan, Russia. The crew conducts research in zero-gravity conditions. Back on earth, scientists discovered how to replace an egg's nucleus with that of a donor, so that an embryo could be born as an identical clone of the donor of the nucleus.

Controversy has erupted over cloning – many want it banned because they feel it diminishes the value of life. Others argue that it can save lives by creating organs that are 100 % compatible with a donor.

## Events

**2000** A long-term crew take up residence in the International Space Station for the first time. Photos from the Mars space probe, *Global Surveyor*, show evidence of water sometime in the planet's past.

**2000** War erupts in Kosovo when ethnic Albanians are massacred by the Serbian army. NATO launches air strikes on Belgrade.

**2001** Al-Qaeda terrorists fly hijacked Boeing 747s into the World Trade Centre in New York, killing almost 3000 people.

**2002** The Larsen B ice shelf in Antarctica collapses.

**2003** US-led troops invade Iraq. Saddam Hussein flees, but is eventually captured.

**2004** A tsunami (tidal wave) triggered by a massive undersea earthquake in the Indian Ocean devastates the shores of Thailand, Indonesia, Sri Lanka and India, killing over 100,000 people.

## What's the big idea? TISSUE ENGINEERING

*Researchers implanted a prototype human ear made of polyester fabric and human cartilage cells onto the back of a hairless mouse. The mouse's tissue nourished the ear while the cartilage grew to replace the fibre. Scientists hope this new technology, called 'tissue engineering', will someday help them to grow external and internal organs for transplants.*

# Inventions

**2000** Wireless communication enters a new era with the introduction of third generation (3G) technology and broadband data services.

**2001** Therapeutic cloning for research is made legal in Britain. British embryologist Ian Wilmut of the Roslin Institute in Scotland created the first cloned mammal - a sheep named Dolly - in 1997.

CCTV in operation

**2001** Following the events of September 11th, the world has grown more security-conscious, and closed circuit TV surveillance systems now operate in most towns and cities.

**2002** Mobile phones now offer a wide range of other functions – storing information, sending and receiving e-mail and Internet access, as well as text, picture and video messaging.

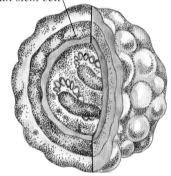

**2003** Fingerprint and optical scanners (left) identify a person by their physical or behavioural features. This is preferred to passwords and PINs, which can be forgotten, stolen or lost.

**2004** The world's largest-ever commercial airliner, the Airbus A380, is unveiled. This twin-deck, four-aisle 'superjumbo' can carry up to 555 passengers, and will enter airline service in 2006.

# Inventors

### Ann Tsukamoto (born 1952)

American Ann Tsukamoto is the co-patentee of a process to isolate the human stem cell (below). Stem cells occur in bone marrow and are the foundation for the growth of red and white blood cells. Understanding how they grow, or could be artificially reproduced, has become vital to cancer research. Tsukamoto's work has led to great advances in understanding the blood systems of cancer patients.

*human stem cell*

### Ian Wilmut (born 1944)

Professor Ian Wilmut was the first scientist to clone a mammal – a Dorset lamb named Dolly – from adult cells. Professor Wilmut's studies pushed cloning into the headlines and roused heated discussion on the ethics and applications of this research. He continues his work with the goal of producing animals that can provide valuable human proteins, which are costly and difficult to produce in large amounts.

61

# Glossary

**Adhesive** Something that sticks things together.

**Almanac** A tabulated list of data.

**Aqueduct** A structure used to transport water.

**Archimedean screw** A tool used to raise water from a river.

**Assembly** A group of people gathered together for a common reason, such as religion or government.

**Asteroid** A type of minor planet that orbits the sun.

**Astronomy** The study of the stars and outer space.

**Atom** The smallest part of an element that can take part in a chemical reaction.

**Barometer** An instrument for measuring atmospheric pressure to predict weather changes.

**Binomial** Having two names.

**Bitumen** A natural substance used on early photographic plates.

**Bubonic plague** An infectious and often deadly disease spread by rat fleas.

**Caravel** A two- or three-masted sailing ship used in the fifteenth and sixteenth centuries.

**Cartographer** Someone who designs and draws maps.

**Cloning** The copying of cells or organisms on a genetic level.

**Contraceptive** A means of preventing pregnancy.

**Cosmonaut** The Russian word for astronaut.

**DNA** The building block of genetic make-up and the characteristics that are passed from parents to children.

**Domesticated** Wild animals under human control.

**Donor** Someone who gives something.

**Dynasty** A line of rulers who are related, such as a father and son.

**Embryo** An animal or human in the early form of development after being conceived.

**Fermenting** Converting sugar to alcohol through a chemical reaction with yeast.

**Flint** A hard form of quartz that occurs in chalk.

**Generator** A machine that creates electrical energy from mechanical energy.

**Habitable** A place that can be lived in.

**H-bomb** The hydrogen bomb, a more powerful version of the atomic bomb.

*Homo erectus* Early man who first walked upright on two feet.

*Homo sapiens* The scientific name for modern man.

**Hydraulic** Operated by water pressure.

**Laser** A narrow beam of high-intensity radiation.

**Leukaemia** A disease that affects the blood.

**Nomadic** People with no fixed home who travel around to find pasture and food.

**Nucleus** The central part of an atom.

**Paleolithic** The period when prehistoric man first made tools.

**Papyrus** Ancient type of paper made from stems of a river plant.

**Pharaoh** An Ancient Egyptian ruler.

**Precursor** Somebody or something that precedes another.

**Prototype** A test model of a new product.

**Protozoans** An organism made up of only one type of cell.

**Psychiatrist** A medical doctor who treats mental illness.

**Psychoanalysis** The study of mental disorders by investigating the role of the unconscious mind.

**Radar** A method for detecting the position and speed of a distant object such as an aircraft.

**Radiotherapy** The treatment of disease, with radiation.

**Sextant** An instrument used for navigating at sea, using the planets to work out direction.

**Shaduf** A counterweight mechanism for raising water.

**Supersonic** Travelling faster than the speed of sound (approximately 1200 km/h).

**Stylus** A pointed writing tool.

**Transformer** A device that transfers current from one circuit to another.

**Transistor** A device that can increase a current.

**Uroscopy** Examination of urine for medical reasons.

**Vaccine** A weakened form of disease given to a patient to make the body produce anti-bodies, which protect the body against more serious diseases.

**Vacuum** A space containing nothing, not even air.

**Ventriloquist** Someone who can produce sounds that seem to come from elsewhere.

# Index

© The Salariya Book Company Ltd MMV
All rights reserved. No part of this book may be reproduced,
stored in a retrieval system or transmitted in any form or by any
means, electronic, mechanical, photocopying, recording or
otherwise, without the written permission of the copyright owner.

Published in Great Britain in 2005 by
Book House, an imprint of
**The Salariya Book Company Ltd**
25 Marlborough Place
Brighton BN1 1UB

ISBN 1 904642 56 X

Please visit the Salariya Book Company at:
**www.salariya.com**

A catalogue record for this book is available
from the British Library.
Printed and bound in China.
The Salariya Book Company operates an environmentally
friendly policy wherever possible.

Editors: Charlene Dobson, Penny Clarke
Illustrated by David Antram, Mark Peppé, John James, Mark
Bergin, Carolyn Scrace, Gerald Wood, Tony Townsend,
Nick Hewetson, Mark Peppé, Bill Donohoe, Ray and Corrine
Burroughs, Hans Wiborg-Jenssen

Visit our website at **www.book-house.co.uk**
for free electronic versions of:
**You wouldn't want to be an Egyptian Mummy!**
**You wouldn't want to be a Roman Gladiator!**
**Avoid joining Shackleton's Polar Expedition!**

Due to the changing nature of internet links, the Salariya Book
Company has developed an online list of websites related to the
subject of this book. This site is updated regularly. Please use this
link to access the list:
**http://www.salariya.com/bp/bigidea**